Imprimatur-Nihil Obstat
Archbishop Tony Scuderi, NOSF, DD, JCD, PsyD, DMin.
Nuncio for the United States of America and Her Territories
Metropolitan Archbishop of California
Minister Provincial for the New Order of St. Francis and Clare (NOSF)
The Interjurisdictional Catholic Church of Christ-Worldwide

©2022 by *Archbishop Tony Scuderi, NOSF,DD,JCD, PsyD,DMin.*

No part of this book may be copied or transmitted in any manner without the expressed permission of Archbishop Scuderi. Permissions may be obtained at bishoptonyscuderi@gmail.com. Any copyright violations will be prosecuted to the fullest extent of the law.

Interjurisdictional Canon Law
Volume 4
Sacraments, Sanctions, and Process Issues
Table of Contents

Preface 7

Chapter 1: How to litigate with diverse churches: The Interjurisdictional Process......................................10

    The Principles of Litigation...........................17

    Developing a Strategy..................................20

    Procedures and Evidence.............................22

    The Essentials..24.

    Thick-skinned is the way to go!..............................24

    Work Harder and Smarter.............................26

    Justice for Cause...28

    The Ethical Interjurisdictional Lawyer...............29

Chapter 2: Validity and Liceity in regard to all the Sacraments except Matrimony and Holy Orders: Introduction..........32

    What is an Impediment?...35

    What is an Irregularity?..35

    The Concept of Validity and Liceity...................36

    How to Fix an Illicit Sacrament........................40

    How to Fix an Illicit (Illegal) Act.......................41

63 The Sacrament of Baptism: Definition and Description..42

    The Minister...47

    The Invalidity, or Illicitness Relevant to the Sacrament of Baptism……………………………………………..48

        Some Examples of Possible Charges………..52.

        Possible Reconciliations and Dispositions…..53

        Appeals if Relevant.................................54

The Sacrament of Confirmation………………………….....55

    A Brief Definition of the Sacrament of Confirmation…56

    The Minister of the Sacrament of Confirmation……….57

    The Form and Matter of the Sacrament of Confirmation………………………………………………….57

        The Invalidity, or Illicitness Relevant to the Sacrament of Confirmation…………………….58

        Charges……………………………………..60

        Possible Reconciliations………………………….61

        Dispositions and Appeals if Relevant………....62

        The Sacrament of Reconciliation (Confession)..63

        The Minister of the Sacrament…………………..65

        The Form of the Sacrament of Reconciliation...68

        The Matter of the Sacrament of Reconciliation……………………………………………..68

        Charges and Appeals Regarding Illicit & Invalid Acts…………………………………..68

The Sacrament of the Holy Eucharist……………………….73

- The Form of the Sacrament of Holy Communion...76

- The Matter of the Sacrament of Holy Communion...77

- Illicit and Invalidating Acts........................77

- Possible Reconciliations for Violations Against the Sacrament of the Holy Eucharist..............79

- Dispositions and Appeals...........................81

The Sacrament of Anointing of the Sick: Definition of the Sacrament of the Anointing of the Sick................................81

- The Form of the Sacrament of the Anointing of the Sick..82

- The Matter of the Sacrament of the Anointing of the Sick..84

- Illicit and Invalid uses of the Sacrament of the Anointing of the Sick................................84

- Possible Reconciliations for Violations against the Sacrament of the Anointing of the Sick.......86

- Dispositions and Appeals...........................87

Chapter 3: Irregularities and Impediments: The Sacraments of Holy Orders (Deaconate, Presbyterate, Episcopacy) and Matrimony- Impediments and Irregularities........................89

- Impediments.. 90

- The Sacrament of Holy Matrimony (Marriage)...92

- Impediments Defined: The Diriment Impediment...94

Akers Chart of Collateral &Linear Relatives with Degree of Kinship: Figure 1......................102

The Introduction of Customs as an Impediment..103

Impediments to Marriage derived from Divine Law vs. Ecclesiastical Law
(a brief clarification)................................105

Table of Consanguinity-Figure 2.................110

Consanguinity Calculations Illustrated 111

Affinity..112

    How it works..............................112

Another example of how affinity works........113

Public Propriety.......................................113

Adoption...114

Spiritual Relationship..............................115

Chapter 4: The Sacrament of Holy Orders-The Effect of the Sacrament of Holy Orders...122

    General Definitions of Holy Orders.............123

    The Permanent Diaconate..........................124

    The Transitional Diaconate........................126

    The Form of the Sacrament........................127

    The Matter of the Sacrament.......................128

    Impediments, and Irregularities Relevant to the Sacrament of Holy Orders to the Diaconate...128

        Part 1: Impediments......................129

    Faith Traditions that Demand a Celibate
    Clergy...130

    Irregularities to Holy Orders......................131

    The Irregularities Affiliated with Mental
    Illness..133

    The Irregularities After Ordination to the
    Priesthood...137

    Simple Impediments Blocking Ordination.....138

Chapter 5: Dispensation Procedures.................................140

    Procedures to Dispense an
    Irregularity(Impediment)...........................141

    Dispensing in the External Forum...............141

    Dispensing in the Internal Forum................144

    In Conclusion..148

    References..149

    Canon Law Dictionary to Volume 4.............157

Preface

This is the fourth volume in the series of Interjurisdictional Canon Law. Up to this point, we have considered the Role of the Canon Lawyer, The Evolution of Canon Law, The concept of time, Lacuna Legis, Customs, General Decrees, Administrative Acts, Persons, Governance, Church and Structure, The development of the Canons as are seen through the development of Roman Law where it all started, The acquisition of real property, Titles and positions, Care of the Soul, The laity, the Clerical state, and other topics. This volume will detail the Sacraments, Sanctions, and Process Issues but only in the Ecclesiastical sense. Our next series will deal with the Civil laws needed that join Canon Law.

In the Sacramental section, we will discuss the 7-Catholic Sacraments. We will discuss the appropriate means to dispense the sacrament, who is to dispense the sacrament and what types of issues may arise canonically, and how to begin to solve the issues.

From the Sacraments, we will move into General Offices and Penalties. This begins with the Interjurisdictional Lawyers job description (if you will). In this section, we will deal with the uniformity of the law and developmental cautions. Types of Penalties will be discussed as an introduction to the penal phase of law once a law is violated. A more intense look will concern itself with the Penalties, Precepts, and Law. As we look at this, I will highlight some of the Roman laws in the Code of Canon Law of 1983 and how they may apply to diverse laws interjurisdictionally, and how the lawyer should approach these issues if a violation in a particular denominations code of canon law is violated.

A good number of Catholic churches have attached to the religious orders and communities. Even though they normally have their particular laws and rules governing them, their independent church cannons do apply to the orders within that denomination and therefore need consideration.

The faithful are also considered in this text. The faithful are just as bound to their church's canons as are their clergy. We will discuss how this works as we look at the Sacraments and interactions with fellow Catholics in their church. We will look at how to proceed if the faithful violate the law and how to disseminate penalties under the law.

The Concept of *Imputability* (the sanity) of a person as they are both deposed and adjudicated. Again, turning to the Roman Code of 1983 as it applies to the outlying independent Catholic churches, we will look at the insanity plea, diminishing capacity, and other imputable offenses.

Upon completing that discussion, we will move into the Censures under the law, Expiatory Penalties, and the application of penalties through the eyes of the Interjurisdictional lawyer and court system. This section discusses the penalty phase of an ecclesiastical trial. To get an understanding of the penalty phase, we must understand the role of the judge and the authority to impose penalties. Again, we look to Rome for insights on how to define this for the Interjurisdictional Judge or Justice.

Since this is a "Church" legal system, we will discuss how crimes and punishments can be treated on diverse levels from the absolution of the crime and penalty to complete excommunication from the church itself and other severities of penalties under the law. This will include what a criminal act looks like, and the penalties associated with the actions.

We must not forget in our discussion's violations against the clergy and the church, and the penalties associated with each of them. This will include subjects ranging from physical or verbal assault on the clergy, doctrinal violations and abuses, clubs and organizations that are affiliated with a church, and much more.

As this text closes, the final chapters will deal with Slander and Libel with special attention paid to the accusations of falsehoods and personal violations of those under sacred vows.

Once this text is concluded, the student should have a very good understanding of how Canon Law works and is to be used and adjudicated.

Chapter 1

How to litigate with diverse churches: The Interjurisdictional Process

Simply put, litigation means filing a lawsuit in a court of law. There are numerous reasons why people file lawsuits. Typically, there are very specific issues that arise in one's state of affairs. For the Canon Lawyer, states of affairs can be rather complicated depending on the situation. For example, it can be a parishioner filing a complaint against her priest for allegedly absconding funds from the church coffers to removing a Presiding Bishop who no longer can function but insists that he or she is just fine. Regardless of the case, it is the disputation of a situation.

According to Grant Killoran (2022), *"Litigation offers certain advantages. Access to the decision-maker, whether judge or jury, is free of charge, except for minimal filing fees.* **Discovery** *is part of the litigation process and can be wide-ranging, allowing the parties to gather a great deal of information. Third parties can be added to a lawsuit, if appropriate. The* **rules of evidence and procedure** *are well defined. The final decision can be enforced by the court. If a party loses, that party has the right to appeal. And litigation does not prevent the parties from attempting ADR* **(Alternate Dispute Resolution)** *or negotiating a settlement before, during, or even after trial"*.

According to Black's Law Dictionary (2009), **discovery** is defined, *in a general sense, as the ascertainment of that which was previously unknown; the disclosure or coming to light of what was previously hidden; the acquisition of notice or knowledge of given acts or facts;*

as , in regard to the "discovery" of fraud, affecting the running of the statutes of limitations, or the granting of a new trial for newly "discovered" evidence. Parker v. Kuhn, 21 Neb. 413, 32 N.W. 74, 59 Am.Rep. 852. Howton v. Roberts, 49 S.W. 340, 20. Ky. Law Rep. 1331.

Discovery, therefore, is the process of gathering evidence and preparing it for presentation in a case, either in a courtroom or through adjudicatory review by a church administrator or legal appointee. The purpose is to ascertain the guilt or innocence of a defendant who has been challenged by the plaintiff and charged with a canonical violation. Part of the process involved in what is called the *discovery phase of the trial* is the gathering of evidence and presenting that evidence in court.

In any case, regardless of if it is a civil case or an ecclesiastical case, the utmost premise is being fair to both the *Victim* (**an individual who has suffered direct physical, emotional, or economic harm as a result of the commission of a crime**.) and the *defendant* (**The person defending or denying; the party against whom relief or recovery is sought in an action or suit. (Black, 2009); A person or group against whom a criminal or civil action is brought (Merriam-webster.com, Retrieved 2022).** Part of the protection of both *parties (defendant and plaintiff)* is the gathering of *Evidence* (**Any species of proof, or probative matter, legally presented at the trial of an issue, by the act of the parties and through the medium of witnesses, records, documents, concrete objects, etc., for the purpose of inducing belief in the minds of the court or jury as to their contention (Black, 2009))**. This phase is called the *Evidentiary phase*. There are rules involved in the gathering and presenting of evidence that will be discussed at a later time.

Before a trial occurs it is best to have an *Alternate Dispute Resolution (ADR)*. According to the Legal Information Institute (Retrieved, 2022), *Alternate Dispute Resolution ("ADR") refers to any method of resolving disputes without litigation. ADR regroups all processes and techniques of conflict resolution that occur outside of any governmental authority. The most famous ADR methods are the following: mediation, arbitration, conciliation, negotiation, and transaction.*

An ADR helps both defendant and plaintiff to find an amicable and admissible solution to their conflicts, disagreements, allegations, and other issues outside the courtroom or tribunal system if in the ecclesiastical realm.

Negotiation is one form of ADR. Negotiations in the church occur between the administrator (hierarchy) and the defendant. There is no pressing need for a canon lawyer, but one may be used if requested for council. Negotiation is not litigation. It is an intervention that helps both parties to agree. Furthermore, it is not mediation or conciliation. The purpose of mediation or conciliation is to promote an amicable between both parties which differ from an intervention.

Another ADR is *arbitration*. Usually, in the ecclesiastical sense, arbitration occurs on the parochial level between an employee of the church and the church (non-clergy personnel unless the clergyperson is an employee of the church and on the payroll of the church such as a secretary, or office manager, etc. An assistant pastor, pastor, or permanent deacon does not qualify under arbitration statutes or laws unless the denominations canon has specific canons addressing this issue). In arbitration, *"the third party (an arbitrator or several arbitrators) will play an important role as it will render an 'arbitration award' (final judgment or decision usually in the form of a declaration that one party owes another money. An arbitrator can also be a judge) that will be binding on the parties (Legal Information Institute, Retrieved, 2022).* ADR differs from conciliation and mediation. In *Arbitration,* a binding decision is imposed by the third party (the arbitrator), whereas in conciliation and mediation, there is no imposition of a binding decision.

In a summation, *Alternate Dispute Resolution (ADR)* is the settling of a dispute outside the courtroom and usually includes a neutral evaluation of each party's testimonies, arguments, and requests. Included as a part of an ADR are negotiations, conciliation, mediation, and arbitration.

Negotiation is what is the "preeminent mode of dispute resolution" (Legal Information Institute, Retrieved, 2022). Discussion and diplomacy are always acceptable means of conflict resolution. It allows both parties, sometimes with a coach or trained negotiator to voice their concerns and requests with one another and come to an amicable solution to the issue. Negotiation is advantageous in that it allows both parties to control the process at the moment. It does not have to be in a formal setting, is flexible, and keeps things out of the courtroom.

Another informal alternative to litigation is *Mediation* which utilizes the services of a trained negotiator. The object of *Mediation* is to bring opposing parties together in an attempt to work out a settlement or agreement that both parties, after discussions, either accept or reject and, if rejection happens, then present alternate ideas, debate, and consider the ideas. *Mediation* can be quite effective in cases that are more dispute-based as opposed to what may be considered felonious or extraordinary in nature such as censures, or excommunications. If there is a disagreement between a pastor and a parishioner or a misunderstanding between clergy and the Ordinary, *Mediation* can be of great assistance.

The final method is *Arbitration*. Arbitration is more formal than mediation but is very similar to court proceedings. It involves a limited discovery phase and the rules of evidence, to be discussed at a later time, are streamlined. For example, one of the terms we will be discussing in evidence is called *hearsay evidence* which is *"an out-of-court statement offered to prove the truth of whatever it asserts"* (Legal Information Institute, Retrieved, 2022). During regular court proceedings, *hearsay evidence* is not allowed to be brought into the testimony (inadmissible). In *Arbitration* hearsay evidence is allowed. In Civil Law, there are different forms of *Arbitration* which we will not discuss here since the diversities do not apply. The concern here is *Ecclesiastical Arbitration* and the use of an arbitrator strictly for canonical and church matters.

The key to arbitration is that a decision is done by process. The arbitrator or panel of arbitrators (not the tribunal) decides the outcome of the arbitration. Though helpful, the arbitrator need not be an Interjurisdictional Canon Lawyer, but does need to be trained in arbitration and is usually chosen to be an arbitrator based on the situation of concern. In other words, if arbitration is needed that concerns finances, it may be a good idea to have an arbitrator trained in financial matters, like a CPA or financial auditor who understands the ins and outs of the issue rather than someone that does not understand the issues at hand. After the arbitration, the arbitrator(s) takes time to review the evidence (deliberate) and then decides (a ruling) on the issue that is binding. The opinions of the arbitrator are not made public but are written and kept usually with the arbitrator and in a specific office file with the Holy See, Chancery, or other designated place where records are kept and maintained. The hierarchy concerned with the case may see and read the documents, but the documents are never to be placed in the public record. All documents made are sensitive and are to be treated in secrecy.

For more information on Civil arbitration refer to U.S. Code Title 9 at the Legal Information Institute's website https://www.law.cornell.edu/uscode/text/9.

Litigation is different. Markham (2006) states, *"The wiser litigators, humbled by the experience and the wiser for it, will rightly tell you that there is no one successful approach to litigating a case and that each litigator must cultivate his own style and methods, making the most of his natural strengths and the best of the besetting weaknesses."* There is a reason why it is called *practicing law* or *having a law practice*. Law is an ever-evolving discipline. It is both an art and a science. Any good artist or scientist will tell you that they must practice their craft daily, and even with all that practice, it still may not be perfect. Law is evolutionary and all the lawyers can expect is to practice what was learned in the classroom and internships and clerkships, find your style, incorporate your style in what was learned and give it the best shot you could in the courtroom, or for that matter, out of the courtroom.

Good lawyers master the subject matter, listen intensely to the client, and take copious notes. Listen not only to what the client is saying but more importantly listen to what the client is not saying. Interpolate what the verbal and non-verbal through a scrupulous review of your notes and apply what you have learned in law school and attempt to present the best defense or prosecution that you can and hope for the best. A good Interjurisdictional litigator will have an excellent understanding of the canons in the church that he is litigating. Know the laws of evidence, courtroom process, and procedure, interviewing skills and techniques, and the paperwork involved. Gather the evidence, organize the evidence, know your counterpart on the other side of the desk and be prepared to give the best characterization of the case honestly and powerfully. The other issue that will arise is that there will be times when you will be attacked (hopefully only verbally) but the opposition. You may be made to feel incompetent, stupid, misinformed, and useless. Have a thick skin! Unless you truly are all of these, understand that this is all part of the game, and you really cannot allow yourself to be caught up in the politics of the situation. Present the facts in evidence, defend, and fight for those facts, and stay the course. As Markham (2006) says, *"Do all these things well, and you will have become a masterful litigator."*

The Principles of Litigation

Know thyself and what thou are about to do. Do it with veracity, intent, power, and accuracy (Scuderi, 2022, Vol 4). You are a lawyer! You are trained in legal principles, processes, and procedures, as well as how to advise your clients concerning their canonical issues and resolutions to those issues regardless of the outcome. If you do the best you can and the case is lost, it probably is not due to what you did wrong. It may be the day, the jury, or there is no other solution except to lose the case because the charge was so heinous that the best that can be hoped for is a settlement, lesser charge, or penalty without a fine.

As a Canon Law attorney understand that your client, regardless of if they are a cleric or not, you are to assume they know little about their particular law. Query them about their understanding of their case and the processes involved until the final disposition is made. As you query, teach, and advise. Get to know your client intimately. There should be "no skeletons" in the closet. The simplest thing that may appear to be unimportant may turn out to be the most important.

Next in the principal process is once you have learned the seriousness of the charges against your client, ask yourself the question, " is there a way I can negotiate a settlement without my client getting excommunicated or censured?" Prepare the defense and understand all the legal forms that need to be completed for the case to be litigated and tried.

The client needs sound representation in any of their legal disputes. This means that you must be prepared to represent the client if the case can be resolved out of court or goes to full litigation. If it goes to full litigation, expect to spend many hours researching, talking on the phone and in person, and be very careful about what you say, when you say it, where you say it, how you say it, and always go in with the thought that no matter where you are gathering evidence or testimony it is being filmed or recorded. Many United States Presidents have been caught off guard and embarrassed by the press because they thought their microphones were turned off when in fact they were not. Remember also, that whatever you write and send out, it does not matter if it is a handwritten note or letter that is stamped and placed in a mailbox, or a text, email, tweet, or any form of cyber media it can be traced, read, discovered and in a good number of instances may be misread or misinterpreted. Regardless of the discovery method, you are responsible for every letter in every word that you speak, write, or send. Representing your client in any legal dispute is called, *Litigation*.

This writer likes the term that Markham (2006) uses, *transactional attorneys*. According to Markham (2006), they are *"supposed to specialize in the first two kinds of work (consultation and performing transactions), while so-called "litigators" or "trial attorneys" are supposed to specialize in the third kind of work (representing clients in disputes that are mediated, litigated, or arbitrated). A good transactional attorney must have a thorough understanding of how a lawsuit proceeds, so that each of his transactions usefully protects the client as much as possible from the hazards of the different kinds of litigation that might one day arise from the transaction, and likewise, a good litigator must have a thorough understanding of the substantive laws that govern the underlying controversy, or else he is operating in the dark, relying solely on his tactical skills or mastery of evidence or perhaps his photogenic charm, but without a fundamental understanding of what the law has to say about the subject at hand."*

The word *transaction* for our purposes needs to be defined. Normally, a transaction concerns some form of fiduciary movement. For us, the word *transaction* though it could apply to finances, will, at this moment, be defined as *any interactions between two or more people.* The actions can range in type and meaning. That said, the Interjurisdictional Lawyer needs to be able to define what the canons of the denomination(s) involved say about the controversy at hand. You must hear and attend to arguments from both sides of the table and gather evidence and proof that support your opinions and case. You must be willing to also, openly, and humbly, hear the other side. What evidence do they bring? How damning is that evidence to your client? Does that evidence have a basis in canon law and if so what is that basis and can you protect your client based on the evidence presented? How will you protect your client? Be futuristic. This means looking into the future and speculating what you think the outcome will be. You and your client should be apprised of all possible outcomes and be willing to accept the outcome and be prepared to take the next steps involved.

By attending to details and listening attentively to the verbal and non-verbal cues of your client, you as a litigator should be able to accurately recognize the type of controversy that is in litigation. Grasp the essentials of the case from day one. Do not wait for day 2, by then it may be too late. The more time that passes the more a case can become convoluted and harder to gather evidence and litigate. Since no one is a mind reader or prognosticator, one cannot be certain of the outcome for any case. Just do the very best you can with your training, research, and skills. This writer believes that *failure is not a failure as we understand it. Failure is a process of learning how to do things just a little bit better, and success is not to be measured by the wins we have, but by the learnings, we acquire to be better for the next time.*

Developing a strategy

In any form of litigation, the attorney must have a strategy going into the case. The first thing is to make sure you say or even think, anything derogatory about the case. Consider that everything you say, regardless of your relationship with the client, will be recorded, or if you are in person, will be videoed and put on social media. Be very careful about this issue. The attorney must be prepared to both win and lose. In both instances not only preparation is mandatory, but follow-up. For example, if the attorney wins the case, what happens after the win? Do they shake hands, the defendant writes the check, and they go their merry ways? Closure must occur. However, whether the attorney decides to do this is up to him or her, but even though the case has been litigated and *disposed of* there needs to be a type of closure and there may even be other things needed to be done. If the case is lost, then the attorney needs to prepare the offender with sound advice and decide what the next plan of action will be if any. Will the attorney appeal? Will the attorney ask for a retrial or attempt to declare a mistrial? How will the attorney prepare the offender for the penalty phase of the trial and the consequences to follow? Again, this all falls on the attorney to develop a strategy and put closure on the case.

The summarization or characterization of the client's situation must be examined closely so that the canon laws that exist, or a variation to them as the court defines, can successfully be applied to the case, and used appropriately for the defense of the client or the prosecution of the client. If used properly a re-characterization of the case may occur giving one or the other an edge in the final disposition of the case which is extremely important, especially in the penalty phase of the trial. The work involved in this portion, and in the preparation and delivery of the case is both tedious and extremely difficult especially, *"if the opposing lawyer is doing precisely the same thing, but in the opposite direction (Markham, 2006).*

Even if the opposing attorney is good at his or her job, their success is most questionable unless you drop your guard and the opposing attorney is more proficient in the understanding of the denomination's laws, read up on similar cases and their final dispositions, the legal procedures they engaged in and the evidence they gathered. Even if challenged, they and you must be thick-skinned and never, ever question your work even if the opposing counsel attempts to discredit you, as you must do to discredit the opposing attorney. Persevere and stay true to the testimony of your client and the denomination's canons as they apply to your defense.

Procedures and Evidence

Courtroom procedures are extremely important and necessary in the understanding of how to proceed with the presentation of evidence in a courtroom. The attorney must have a grasp of not only the law of the particular church's canons but must have an underlying strategy on how to approach the court and present their case. If the attorney does not have the basics, the attorney has nothing and needs to go back to school or resign! Telling your client's story and applying that story to the law is of utmost importance and imperative. This will draw out the evidence in the case and illustrate the truth dispelling any spurious notions by the other side. Through the application of the law adjunctive to the testimony of the client, the storyline becomes proven by the evidence presented. If the research is not done and a tightly woven *preponderance of the evidence* is not presented then what is presented is mere conjecture and will lose the case. The evidence provided will stand on its own accord and provide the necessary evidence to either exonerate or accuse the defendant. You, as the attorney, must have evidence that supports the testimony of the defendant, or you have no case, and you will lose and most probably be embarrassed.

The Interjurisdictional Canon Lawyer must understand the procedures involved in the gathering of and present of the evidence. How the evidence is obtained is of grave importance and a necessity in the prosecution or defense of a case. One small error in evidence gathering will lose the case even if the defendant is innocent. Once the evidence is gathered, organized, synthesized, and prepared in a courtroom brief, the presentation of the evidence is the next paramount process. Through the understanding of the *Laws of Evidence,* you will be able to have your evidence admitted and the opposing council's evidence either sequestered, nullified, or not admitted (deemed inadmissible). Remember, however, that the opposing counsel will be doing the same thing to depose and denigrate your evidence.

The only way to master the skills of litigation is to prepare, present and practice-practice-practice. Do not be afraid to not have the outcome the way you wish it to be. If you put this ahead of the evidence or the good of the client, you will surely fail, and rightly so. If you do what you are trained for and do not succeed, it is not, as was written above, viewed in this writer's opinion as a failure, but a growth lesson that hopefully will not repeat itself. If you believe in the law of the church you are defending or prosecuting and believe in the defendant or plaintiff, and follow all the guidelines governing the judicial process, with the proper practice, success will follow.

The Essentials

One of the questions that must be asked is, What is a sound litigation strategy? To respond to this question a thorough understanding of the substantive canon law governing the matter presented to the court and the council must occur, and it must jibe with what your client presents to you. If it does not the case comes into question and so does the gathered evidence. Having said this, the presentation of a clear, concise, and complete summarization of the facts in evidence is necessary. Adjoining this is the solid application of the canon law to which the case applies. This will provide for, hopefully, a favorable outcome for you and the client.

If the Interjurisdictional Canon Lawyer skillfully and crafts the appropriate litigation tactics applicable to the case at hand along with the rules of evidence to pull together the evidence in the discovery phase of the trial, then organize that evidence, properly present it to prove your case, and remove, or exclude the other council's evidence the case is yours.

Thick-skinned is the way to go!

Having a "Thick-Skin" does not intimate that you do not pay attention to what the opposition has to say or does to you. The key is for the lawyer, regardless of what side you are on, to be able to tolerate the impudence and attacks from the other side, and/or if the case is in the public forum, for example, if the case involved child molestation or sexual assault, from the public and media.

Adversity, insults, and inaccurate reporting are just a few scenarios that may purport derision and malcontent. There will also be indifference and disapproval for what you are doing to defend or prosecute the individual. Be mindful of these and other incendiary insults and actions from the opposition, be they attorneys or the public forum. If you are an individual that lacks the propensity to disregard such behaviors and verbal inappropriateness, do not become a litigator. The key is never to respond, positively or negatively to the incendiary comments. Always remain neutral and thank those who curse you. One thing this writer has found helpful when responding to negative "press" is to say, *"I hear you, and thank you for your comment. I will consider it. Thank you."* Then just walk away and don't pay attention to anything else. The other thing is not to respond at all, remain silent, and get out of the area as quickly as possible.

The key to adversarial commentaries is to be proactive and not reactive. Even in anger and refutations, there is something to be learned. Those threatening you, for example, might be threatened by you. In psychology, this is called *Projection*. The person feels inadequate within themselves and sometimes rather insecure. Since their ego cannot manage insecurities and inadequacies it either consciously or unconsciously *acts out* and *projects* those uncomfortable feelings onto a receiving object, that would be you. The individual identifies you as the threat. This is called *projective identification*. It can be *covert* (within the person) or *overt* (outside the person). In *projective identification*, it is an overt response.

Therefore, the threat may not be intentional on your part. They may be threatened by your knowledge and prowess along with your accuracy in presenting your case. In other words, their anger and retort are not about you, it is about them and their insecurities and in some cases, their anger or viciousness. If that is the case, that is what this writer calls *narcissistic projective sociopathy* due to their inadequacy. To be a good litigator is to metaphorically be a descent prognosticator (at least the best you can be) and to, as Michelle Obama said, *"when they go low, [sic] you go high."* All cases are to be fought hard and sometimes long. If you wish to win for your client, the parishioner, cleric, bishop, or church, expect to be in it for the long haul. Never let the vicious, poisonous, abhorrent, pugilistic inappropriate attacks and disposition of the opposing counsel or public opinion taint your defense or prosecution of a case, cloud your judgment and your professionalism.

Work Harder and Smarter

As an attorney, you will be up against a lot of opposition, but you will also find it rewarding if you pace yourself, stay the course, and work harder and smarter. Good research of a case and perseverance will be the key to a successful career as an Interjurisdictional Canon Lawyer. Days will turn into nights and nights will turn into weeks. Never be idle. Do your due diligence but pace yourself and care for yourself. You must work hard on each case as if it is your only case. Many hours will be spent reading books, posts, online journals, and articles gathering depositions, writing briefs, practicing your defense or prosecution, and opening and closing statements. Do not be afraid, be careful not to violate any ethical standards or court orders to have your materials reviewed and listened to (if preparing opening and closing statements). If the lawyer is not prepared, the lawyer will surely fail and will not only be embarrassed in the courtroom but if not skilled enough to correct the mistakes made, will not have a long career as an Interjurisdictional Lawyer. Organize yourself, your work, your time, and your caseloads. Understand the cause of your actions and the cause of the disputes and the cause of the circumstances that brought your client to you to either defend or prosecute.

Every litigator that has a record of success attains this through well practiced and developed organizational skills and behaviors. At the outset of a case, start preparing your closing statements. You may think this is idiosyncratic since you may not know everything about the case or how the case will develop. That is the entire point! Treat each step along the way as if you need to present a final summation. As the case proceeds you want to gather your notes and reports along the way and write a summary of each phase from the initial presentation, through deposition, into the evidentiary phase to the summative phase and closing arguments of the case. If you do this correctly and modify your notes and summations as you go along, your case will be airtight, and your summation will be conclusive, poignant, and sound. Even if the final verdict does not go in your favor, you will have presented a well-thought-out, prepared, and tightly knit case. If it does not go well. Learn the places where things fell short and note them. Hopefully, those issues that fell short will not repeat themselves. Nonetheless, if you did the best you can, given your knowledge, expertise, and preparation, there is no need to second guess yourself or question your competence. The last point is to use all resources at your beck and call. This means any form of computerized programs, cyber research, and a team of people, if needed, to assist in the preparation, defense, prosecution, and presentation of your cases.

<u>Justice for Cause</u>

The final important point for the Interjurisdictional Lawyer to understand and practice is that every case you try must be for a just cause. If not, please consider refusing the case because it may borderline on or be a case unethical in nature. Always follow the steps in due process of law. Understand the ecclesiology of the charges. That means not only that what the person did was a breach of canon law but understanding what that person did to undermine the law and offend the church or person(s) will be paramount in case preparation. Also, understand the Church's part in the case. The Church can be one of two things, right or wrong. The Church will approach the offense very cold and calculated holding dearly to their canon law. They will present the canons and the offense to the canons as matter-of-fact. In other words, the offender understood the canons, violated the canon(s), and based on the letter of the canon will prosecute accordingly with very little if any hearsay evidence. Here is the law. Here is how the person violated the law. Therefore, the person will be punished under the law and receive justice under the law based on his or her insubordinate actions to the law. If the Interjurisdictional Lawyer believes there is a way to either usurp, bend, nullify, or negotiate the case for a just cause and not to just get their client "off the hook", the lawyer did his or her due diligence.

The litigators' job is to represent their clients morally, ethically, and professionally in legal disputes remembering always that justice must prevail even if not in your favor. The laws governing the case are presumed to be ever-evolving and revisionist in nature and content. They are not perfect, but they should be just and fair for all. Final dispositions should be based on sensibility, fairness for both parties, and procedurally sound. Statutes must be adhered to, and the case must be decided based on the statutes and violations of those statutes. Penalties are to be meted out fairly and without prejudice and based solely on the evidence presented and interpretation of the evidence and influences that the evidence has on each litigator, judge, or justice and all the parties involved. Litigate fairly. Aggressive litigation does not mean narcissistic, egomaniacal, or out of control demeaning the other side when an opening is available.

The Ethical Interjurisdictional Lawyer

Legal ethics is a subject unto itself. However, at this juncture in time, it may be a good place to point out just a few items. Fairness and equity are not synonymous terms in law. Sometimes what is fair equates to justice under the law whereas, at other times, fairness equates to just laws.

Our discussion starts with the client. Sometimes, after spending hours talking to the client, preparing the case, and hearing the pain and suffering that the client is enduring feelings of having more than a lawyer-client relationship may ensue. If you feel that the relationship is beginning to feel significantly different than the usual lawyer-client relationship and you have a sense that you, the lawyer, are doubling as a friend that is connected with your client on social media, or just building a personal friendship, this may be what is known as a *dual relationship*. There are several types of *dual relationships* that you should be aware of, and we will discuss these at a later time feel free to research them. The attorney should have sufficient enough detachment from his or her client so that a clear assessment of the situation is not clouded by the relationship. This does not mean that the attorney should be completely an automaton. Not at all! Feelings and emotions are what drive a case. You must *join* with the client to champion the cause of the case. If the attorney begins to feel something as the case proceeds, the attorney should not abandon those feelings but find out the meaning of those feelings and use them as a guide to litigate or gather evidence. If it goes nowhere then examine the etiology of those feelings within yourself. Never void yourself of human emotions. Use them to your benefit. Another issue arises when the attorney becomes a stone-cold bureaucrat or traffic officer directing traffic at a busy intersection. There is an old Indigenous People's Saying. To paraphrase it, *never judge another unless you have walked a mile in their moccasins.* For the Interjurisdictional Lawyer, meaning, have empathy, not sympathy, for your client. You can be sympathetic to the cause, feeling sorry for what has happened to get the person where they are at the moment. But that is not empathy. Empathy is a way to metaphorically feel what the patient is feeling through the understanding of your feelings if you were to encounter the same scenario as the client. Regardless of how insignificant you, the Interjurisdictional Lawyer, may believe the client's feelings are, that feeling(s) can be an insurmountable burden on that client that is both paramount and monumental. Understand this and have the common courtesy to acknowledge these feelings as real and accurate measurements of that person's experience at the moment. Even if the feelings are not reality-based, that does not mean they are not real. Consider everything in front of you as a part of the patient's pain and suffering and approach every case with a sense of Justice and moral certitude never allowing any form of ingratitude, indignation, or inappropriate words or actions by opposing council to interfere with your good judgment.

Chapter 2

Validity and Liceity in regard to all the Sacraments except Matrimony and Holy Orders

Introduction

Every Catholic Church with any merit holds as dogma and doctrine that there are seven sacraments, Baptism, Confirmation, Reconciliation, Holy Eucharist, Matrimony, Holy Orders, and Anointing of the Sick.

According to Scott P. Richert, in *Learning Religions: What is a Sacrament, A lesson inspired by the Baltimore Catechism, (2019),* "*A sacrament is a symbolic rite in the Christian religion, in which an ordinary individual can make a personal connection with God – The Baltimore Catechism defines a sacrament as "**an outward sign instituted by Christ to give grace.**" That connection, called **inner grace**, is transmitted to a parishioner by a priest or bishop, who uses a special set of phrases and actions in one of seven special ceremonies."*

There are two parts to the dispensing of any sacrament, the **Form,** and the **Matter**. The best way to think of the **Form** is to think of the word, *Formula*. It is the words that are used by the priest or bishop, and in baptism also the deacon. The **Matter** is the instrument used as an outward sign to confect the sacrament. For example, water is used in Baptism and Holy Chrism is used in Confirmations and Holy Orders. Both water and chrism are the **Matter** of the sacrament.

The importance of the sacraments to the Interjurisdictional Canon Lawyer is to understand that the dispensing of the sacraments must liturgically follow the appropriate ceremony. This includes not only the correct Form and Matter as outlined in each of the Church's Codes of Canon Law but also the use of the correct dispenser of the sacrament (the Deacon, Priest, or Bishop). If the Form, Matter, or Dispenser comes into question this can be a very serious ecclesiastical issue. If, for example, a valid and licit Bishop is not the one who ordains a priest, anything that priest does is invalid and illicit (doesn't count and is illegal according to Canon Law). This causes issues especially if the alleged priest decides to confer the sacrament of matrimony. If he acts as a valid and licit minister of the Gospel, which in this scenario that priest is not, then the entire marriage is invalid. They are not married, and the ceremony must be redone either by a judge, justice of the peace, or a valid and licit priest. We'll address this issue in the chapter on marriage.

Each section of Chapter 2 will be devoted to each individual sacrament. This chapter will give a brief definition of the sacrament in an understandable manner to cover those denominations that may not define the sacrament differently or call it by its name but may not recognize it as a sacrament. Also, to be considered, are the Form and Matter of the Sacrament, the Dispenser of the Sacrament, and what happens if there is an irregularity, impediment, or incorrect Form, Matter, or Minister. The sections will also consider the duties of the Interjurisdictional Canon Lawyer in litigating each of the sacraments.

This chapter will not go into a detailed explanation of the sacraments which is covered in another Volume in the Interjurisdictional series. This section will cover the law incorporating Roman Canon Law, but there will be sections that are not considered in or apply to Roman Law. These are some issues pertinent to the Interjurisdictional Canon Lawyer and should act as an umbrella for all traditions with applicable sacraments.

Each sacrament will be discussed in this manner:

1. The Name of the Sacrament
2. A brief definition/description of the Sacrament
3. The Minister of the Sacrament
4. The Form of the Sacrament
5. The Matter of the Sacrament
6. Impediments, irregularities, etc., relevant to the Sacrament
7. Charges
8. Possible reconciliations
9. Dispositions and Appeals if relevant will conclude this section.

As each sacrament is worked through the process above, keep in mind that the judicial processes may differ from church to church according to the Canon Law of that church. If the law is unjust, unclear, or non-existent, or if the defendant or plaintiff needs representation to plead their case the Interjurisdictional Canon Lawyer may be called upon to litigate the event.

What is an Impediment?

The Roman Catholic Church defines an *Impediment* (CLSA, 1993) an *Impediment* is a legal obstacle that prevents a sacrament from being performed either validly or licitly or both. The term is frequently used when it refers to Marriage and Marriage Law and Holy Orders. Some *impediments* can be removed whereas others cannot. In most cases the local bishop (the Ordinary of the Diocese) can remove an impediment, however, for the most serious ones, only the Holy See or Presiding Bishop may be the only one permissible by Canon Law that is able to remove the impediment.

Even though this is a Roman Catholic definition, some Interjurisdictional denominations that follow or use the Roman Canons as a guideline, define impediment in the same way and for the removal of some, only the head of the church (Primate, Eparch, etc.) can remove the impediment.

The main discussion on Impediments will be in the area of Marriage and only those ordained to the Priesthood. Interjurisdictional Canon Law will apply all impediments discussed to ALL Holy Orders with exceptions to be discussed at that time.

What is an Irregularity?

An *Irregularity* is a perpetual *Impediment*. They are conditions that prevent or *impede* a person from obtaining a particular sacrament or have the effect of the sacrament removed so the person can no longer function in that office. The cause can be a past or present sin, like murder, or a violation of the law like a

Tort (*delicts*). An irregularity can stop someone from obtaining Holy Orders or getting married. It is a permanent condition. If a person receives the sacrament of reconciliation and is absolved. Does the irregularity go away? The answer is, no! The sin is absolved, but the action and effect of that sin hold. For example, if a church says a priest or religious must remain celibate and they have sexual relations and are removed and stripped of their Holy Orders, even if it was a one-time affair and nothing came out of the affair, they can present remorse in the confessional and be forgiven of the sin of fornication, but the action causing the sin cannot be taken back. It is the action that presents the irregularity and therefore the penalty and punishment. If, however, the irregularity is removed ecclesiastically, then the irregularity is *dispensed,* and the person may get ordained or continues as a religious if not in Holy Orders. When deciding if an action will warrant an irregularity always consult with the denominations Code of Canon Law or Legal Documents of similar nature but under a different name like Manifesto, or Constitution.

The main discussion on Irregularities will be in the area of Marriage and only those ordained to the Priesthood. Interjurisdictional Canon Law will apply all impediments discussed to ALL Holy Orders with exceptions to be discussed at that time

The Concept of Validity and Liceity

Two terms that are of extreme importance in any litigation are *Validity* and *Liceity*. They describe the effectiveness of the sacrament that is performed. These two terms draw their definitions and implications from *Impediments and Irregularities*. As this writer reviewed the literature, he could not find a single denomination that did not require sacraments or business actions to be legal (Licit) and take effect (Valid).

Though these two words seem logical and straightforward, in Canon Law they need to be clearly defined and understood.

When *Validity* is discussed and defined the intended effect of the sacrament takes place. If there is an action performed in either *Form* or, *Matter* that can *invalidate* the sacrament (Dictionary: Validity, Retrieved 2022).

An action is said to be *valid* if it has integrity. That is, is it honest, true, and consists of truthfulness. **Example 1.** A valid mass is one that is said by a priest that has been ordained by a bishop and is in good standing with the church with which he or she is affiliated.

When *Liceity* or something is *Licit* that means it is *Lawful* and follows the letter of the law as it is written. It can be tricky when discussing the sacraments, to be a *licit* sacrament because sometimes they can be *valid* and still be *illicit*, but if something is *illicit*, it is always *invalid*. To be *licit* means that the sacrament is performed in the correct manner following the rubrics and canons of the church, in other words, the sacrament did happen. However, if during the performance of the sacrament it was done in a way that is not permissible by Canon Law or other rules of the respective church or denomination that sacrament is *illicit*, it happened but not done in accordance with the norms of the church.

When we talk about a sacrament being *invalid*, this is more serious. If a Sacrament is deemed *invalid* what is actually being said is that it never happened at all. There was a character defect in the performance or dispensation of the sacrament. When dispensing a sacrament, it must be done with the proper *Form* and the one dispensing the sacrament must have proper *Intent*. If either of these is missing the sacrament never happened.

When discussing Validity or Invalidity remember, that it applies ONLY to sacraments and nothing else in Canon Law.

Example 2: Valid vs. Invalid: Mass is said by a validly ordained priest. According to Canon Law, only a priest can do the homily. In this example, a layperson gives the homily. The mass is valid, but the homily was invalid because it was not done by the priest, who, according to the norms of the church dictated by Canon Law, must give the homily.

Example 3: Illicit but Valid: Most priests in the Independent Church movement have been laicized from their denomination. Accordingly, they no longer may enjoy the celebration of or dispense of the sacraments. A Roman Catholic Priest that leaves to get married is dispensed (released) of his obligations as a priest and may no longer celebrate mass, be a deacon of the church, or may not preach, teach, or even hold any form of ministry such as reading at mass or being an extraordinary minister. The only function that a priest may perform is to hear confessions, but, only in dire emergencies. If not an emergency, that priest may not hear confessions. Given this, the definition of *laicization,* If a laicized priest celebrates mass, the mass, by virtue of the indelible mark on the soul of the priest is valid but according to the norms of the church dictated by Canon Law, it is invalid.

Example 4: Illicit but Valid: If that same priest gets excommunicated or if that priest was ordained without the approval of the Presiding Bishop or Head of the church, and celebrates mass, the mass is still valid but illicit for the same reason as in Example 3 above.

Example 5: Completely Invalid: Let us stay on the topic of any priest (valid or not) says mass. Being affiliated with a denomination that broke from Rome (Independent clergy), that priest belongs to a church that sticks by the Roman Canon and tradition that women are not to be ordained. This priest decides to hold a mass with a "new Liturgy" that has not been approved by his or her denomination and during that liturgy ordains a woman to the priesthood.

In this case, the *intent* of the priest was to disrespect and subjugate the Form of the liturgy by creating his own unapproved liturgy using his own From. This is termed *improper intent of form*. During the liturgy, the priest decides, without permission, to use grape juice instead of wine for the consecration. The church, according to its Canon Law insists on the use of wine, unless there is an exception and has been approved by the Ordinary of the Diocese or higher. This is termed *improper intent of matter.* If this same priest's intention was to ordain the woman just to spite the church but did not believe she was ordained, but she believed she was being ordained, besides fraudulent ordination, that in itself nullifies the act, the priest did the ordination with no intention to really ordain the woman. This is termed *improper intention*. In all of these examples what was done was totally invalid. As mentioned above, all invalid sacraments are also illicit. That mass was as if it never happened, and the ordination never happened.

If any sacrament is done *invalidly,* Jesus is not present. If, however, a sacrament is done *illicitly* but is done by a clergyperson who has proper intent and Holy Orders (a valid performance), Jesus is present but not very happy about the event.

If an action is performed by a qualified individual with proper intent and using the essential elements to perform the sacrament according to Canon Law it is considered to be a *valid* act. If an unauthorized sacrament is performed it is considered to be valid by juridic standards, but it is illegal.

How to Fix an Illicit Sacrament

In most cases, fixing an illicit sacrament is easy. Once deemed illicit, for example, using the incorrect Form in baptism by a validly ordained priest, and using something like, *I baptize you in the name of the Creator, the Redeemer and Sanctifier*, That baptism, according to the rubrics stating that the Triune formula, *I baptize you in the name of the Father and of the Son and of the Holy Spirit* must be used, that baptism is invalid. The critical element of Form is not as prescribed. The remedy for this is to re-baptize the person using the correct Form, Matter, and Intent (of course using a validly ordained minister according to the denomination's Code of Canon Law). Most sacraments can be remedied in this manner unless otherwise specified in the Code of Canon Law of that Church.

How to Fix an Illicit (Illegal) Act.

Remember, an *illicit act* is one that is performed outside the law. Baptism is a sacrament that requires the person to either be fully immersed in the water or have water "poured" over the head of the person. If a priest or whomever the code says can baptize a person uses, for example, an *aspergillum (a sprinkler)*, dribbles water on the head in droplets, or dips their hand in the water and sprinkles it on the head, this sacrament is *illicit* and should not be done. Follow the proper form and all is well. This can be perfectly licit if the denomination's code of canon law says that is the practice of that denomination.

Since this is a very critical topic, allow me to reiterate, that *it is impossible to act in a way that is invalid and is still licit. If it is invalid, it is always illicit!* If something is invalid the only fix is to do it over, this time correctly following the law and rubrics.

The reader will see how complicated this can be when we talk about the sacraments of marriage and Holy Orders. For example, if a marriage is valid but illicit, the reason may be due to failing to have the correct permissions to do the sacrament, which makes it illegal, however, the marriage itself, done by an appropriate clergyperson according to law, is valid.

There is not much one can do to fix this. Just make sure in the future that the law is followed as prescribed.

The Sacrament of Baptism

Definition and Description

Every Christian Church has its form of Baptism. Baptism is the gateway sacrament into the church, Christian family, and as an eternal mark on the soul, a child of God welcoming him or her into the kingdom of heaven. That indelible mark on the soul, according to most faith traditions, defines the recipient as a Child of God. This begs the question, then why are other sacraments needed? Some Christian churches have sacraments after Baptism whereas others like the Quaker Religion have no sacraments. Baptism is the first *"Sacrament of Initiation"* welcoming a new person into a particular church.

Redeemer (1996) reminds us that even with the scriptural passages alluding to St. John the Baptist baptizing people in the Jordan, Baptism happened long before John. The Hebrew people used it as a cleansing rite to identify those deemed impure or unclean and performed ceremonial rituals of cleansing. Exodus 19:5-15 talks about ceremonial cleansing which we view today as one of the earliest baptisms (Scuderi, 2022, in A Text, Commentary and Canon Law of the ECCC). There are 17 places in the Bible that clearly state that salvation is gained through faith (they are: Romans 1:17, 3:23-24, 3:27, 3:28, 3:30-31, 4:1,4:2, 4:5,4:16, ,5:1;5:15-17, 1 Corinthians 1:29, 9:21, Genesis 15:16, Habakkuk 2:4, Galatians 2:16, 2:21, 3:24. Justification by faith is mentioned in Heb. 11:4,

Philippians 3:9, Romans 5:1, Heb:10:38, and Habakkuk 2:4 with additional references in Romans 4:3 and Galatians 3:6 (English Standard Version Bible, 2021-all cites above)). Nonetheless, every Christian tradition considers the 8 accounts of John the Baptist baptizing with water including the Baptism of Jesus in Matthew 3:13. It was through this (the Baptism of Jesus) that the churches derived the formula for baptism, *"N. I baptize you in the name of the Father and of the Son and of the Holy Spirit. Amen.* Without this formula, and the matter of water sprinkled on the forehead, theologically the sacrament does not take effect and the person is not baptized. This formula is to be taken strictly with no revisions. It must be said as it is written above in all Christian faiths, or the "Catholic" denominations will not accept that baptism as valid. A question was asked, *I want to become a Baptist, however, I was baptized as an infant in an Orthodox church. Will I be rebaptized when entering the Baptist Church?* The answer found on the Quora website (Retrieved, 5/14/22) was responded to on May 7, 2016, by John Simpson. He gave a rather lengthy explanation that infant Baptism "is not baptism… it's not New Testament baptism." For most Christians this answer is a problem. Once baptized you are forever baptized. There is only one baptism according to Ephesians 4:5 ((English Standard Version Bible, 2021), *We have only one Lord, one faith, one baptism through whom all things came and through whom we exist.*

    As you can see there may be issues with people who have been baptized and a denomination does not want to accept that baptism for one reason or another. Regardless of the rationale being that as an infant the person is unable to decide if that is what they want to do, they forget that is what the sacrament of Confirmation is about. We'll discuss that in a moment. If a person is rejected from a church because they were baptized as a child, and they really want to be a part of that church, that person can legally refute the rejection through the ecclesiastical court in the Interjurisdictional System of law on the scriptural grounds based on Ephesians 4:5.

A church, however, can refuse on legal grounds a prospective parishioner on the grounds that the form of baptism was not correct based on Matthew 3:13. The whole idea of baptism is for the person to be infused for all eternity with the mark of the Holy Spirit as an indelible mark on the soul to protect that person from the evil one.

It rarely comes that someone will want to take a denomination to court for not allowing them into the church because that church will not accept their baptism. Normally, the person may get angry, say a few inappropriate words, and go elsewhere and that is the end of the event. However, if the case does arise it may be a good idea to discuss the matter with church officials to discover their rationale concerning the non-acceptance and go from there.

In Catholic traditions, by virtue of baptism using the appropriate form and matter, who can baptize? This question was asked and answered by Apologetics Press (Retrieved 2022). According to the Press, the place to go for this answer is the New Testament. *"The primary lesson learned is that the personal characteristics of the individual doing the baptizing have no bearing on the effectiveness of the baptism. In other words, it does not matter who does the baptizing, as long as the baptism is a complete immersion in water (Romans 6:4; Acts 8:38), in the proper name (Matthew 28:19; Acts 19:1-9), and for the proper reason (Acts 2:38)."* In 1 Corinthians 14-17 St. Paul intimates that the one baptizing does not make a difference because baptism is based on a relationship to God's overall plan of salvation. So, technically, any baptized Christian can baptize another willing Christian without the assistance of clergy. Imagine the controversy behind that idea. Therefore, most churches in their canon laws define who can and cannot perform valid and licit baptisms. If a person comes to the Interjurisdictional Lawyer with the complaint that a church is being prejudicial against them based on the validity and liceity of their baptism, go to that denomination's code of canon law and review that denomination's criteria for baptism. If it states that only their clergy can baptize, that individual needs to get rebaptized. This does not mean that the first baptism did not take effect. It did! All it means is that a particular church denomination does not recognize the effectiveness of that sacrament.

Certain churches may invalidate a baptism because the rite and ritual were not followed precisely, or a minister proper to their faith tradition was not used for the ceremony. The effect of the sacrament is debatable so long as the correct formula was used. Arguments can be made that if the correct formula as outlined above was used the sacrament is valid and licit. The key is that baptism incorporates the person into the Catholic or Christian faith regardless of the denomination, but only with the proper formula used.

For example, plunging the person into a pool of water or a river three times (symbolizing the Holy Trinity) and saying something like, "in the name of Jesus are you saved?" with the person's response being "Amen, I'm saved," though a nice symbol and gesture is not valid nor licit in most Christian churches and if a person indicates that that is the way he or she was baptized, and wants to argue the case, review the church's canon laws, show them to the person and encourage them to be baptized.

Everything in the sacrament of Baptism to ensure validity and liceity is found in each denomination's Code of Canon Law and should be strictly followed.

According to Scott (2021), *" Baptism celebrates the first initiation of an individual into the church, whether as an infant or as an adult. The rite consists of a priest [sic.] deacon or bishop, pouring water over the head of the person being baptized, as he says, "* **I baptize you in the name of the Father, and of the Son and of the Holy Spirit."**

The Form: The Trinitarian Formula words: " N. I baptize you in the name of the Father and of the Son and of the Holy Spirit" must be used.

The Matter: Water is the main Matter (and in some cases salt), the second Matter but not necessary in cases of emergency or outside of liturgy, Oil of Catechumens, must be used. There can be no exceptions. For example, one cannot baptize with Coca-Cola, Milk, or an Alcoholic Beverage, nor can one just "sprinkle" water. It must be water and must be done either by full immersion or poured over the forehead.

The Minister

The ordinary minister of Baptism is the Deacon, Priest, or Bishop. It is usually under emergency circumstances that a layperson baptizes. Even though by virtue of their Baptism, any layperson may baptize another, that is the exception rather than the norm. There are numerous issues that may arise if a layperson baptizes another. Was the baptizer, baptized him or herself and can they prove it? What Form did they use? Was the Matter correct, did they use water? Were there godparents witnessing? With what church did they baptize since baptism is a welcoming into a church community? Did the baptizer complete paperwork and hand it to the appropriate denomination's administrative offices or church? Was proper intent on both parts used? Was the person free to be baptized and was it of their own free choice if adults and agreed upon by the caregiver if an infant? Was this baptism done in a cult or other inappropriate venue? Was this an emergency and if so, what was the emergency?

If any of the above, and other items found in the Canon Law of the church in question are missing, then it is possible that that baptism was not valid or licit and must be redone according to the rubric of that particular church.

The Invalidity, or Illicitness Relevant to the Sacrament of Baptism.

We can see from the above material that any baptized Christian, and in some cases and churches, a non-baptized person with proper intent and the correct *Matter*, can baptize another willing person and that baptism is valid and licit.

There are, however, several things that may happen for the validity and liceity of the sacrament not to take effect. If, for example, a person does not want to be baptized and the person doing the baptism performs the ritual. For example, let us say a person is very ill and has never been baptized. A Christian goes up to that person, maybe their good friend and both understand that the ill person has little time to live. The friend, knowing that person has never been baptized, asked the person if they want to be baptized because if that individual is not baptized, the friend believes that the friend will never enter the gates of heaven, even if they lived a good life. The ill friend still refuses to be baptized and goes temporarily unconscious. The friend, thinking that the friend will not wake up gets water and uses the proper formula, and baptizes the ill friend. The friend wakes up. Is that person baptized? The family found out about this incident and calls you, the local Interjurisdictional Canon Lawyer, and asks if their loved one who doesn't believe and never wanted to be baptized, is baptized. What do you say to that family? And why did you give that answer?

Remember, in order for a sacrament to take effect, generally speaking, again referring to the denominational canon laws of the particular church, there needs to be consent from that person. The individual cannot be coerced, forced, or threatened. Unless after the baptism was completed using the correct form and the ill person after waking up said it was alright that the person baptized him or her, that sacrament did not take effect. If the person rejects the sacrament or was given a sacrament without their consent, infant baptism included if the parents refuse to have their baby baptized, that will constitute an irregularity and illicit act, and that person would have to get re-baptized later in life if they wanted to be baptized.

Other possible issues, which will be discussed later in this text that can constitute issues surrounding the effect of the sacrament center on the mental status of the person, the understanding of the meaning of the sacrament (Interjurisdictionally this is called, *sacramental ignorance*), and any obstacle to the sacrament as purported in a denominations Code of Canon Law.

Sacramentally there is an issue. It can be argued that if a person who is validly and licitly baptized baptizes another person, even against their will, that person is baptized validly but not licitly. By virtue of the theology behind the effect of the sacrament and the dispenser of the sacrament, it is a valid baptism. However, because the person refused the sacrament or denies the efficacy of the sacrament, it was illegally (illicitly) dispensed. In this case, the sacrament is valid but illicit. If the person is baptized or not depends on the belief of the person and the denomination's canon law. Most importantly, the real question is, does it matter? The answer is that no one knows what is in the mind of God.

Another issue that arises with the validity of Baptism is in the case of those who openly and knowingly know a person has been baptized before validly and licitly and re-baptize that person. If this is the case, then the person performing the baptism becomes the *irregular agent* and the sacrament does not take effect. There is literature that the perpetrators of this form of baptism confer what is known as *conditional baptism* where there is no doubt that the person was already baptized validly and licitly. However, there are canonists that do agree with this concept of *conditional baptism* and a *conditional baptism* is a valid baptism.

If the person being baptized is a known heretic and does not repent, turn away from this sin and embrace the Good News and church doctrine, and allow him or herself to be baptized, this is an impediment, and the sacrament does not take effect. The exception is infant baptism done by heretics. If a heretic was at one time a full believer and member of a Church and baptized validly, then later abandoned the faith, and became a heretic, that person still has the indelible mark on his or her soul as a Baptized Christian. If that person then, for any appropriate reason, an emergency for example, or a catastrophic event, and baptizes an infant, that infant is validly Baptized. Other than that, this is considered an abuse of the Sacrament of Baptism (See Fanning, 1910).

Here is another example of how Rev. Matthew Hood in Detroit caused a lot of problems. Here is the excerpt from **Reese (2020-09-15), in Religious News Services.**

*In June the **congregation**, which deals with doctrinal issues, ruled that a baptism was invalid if the minister said, "We baptize" instead of "I baptize...."*

*This caused absolute chaos in **Detroit**, where the Rev. Matthew Hood saw in a video of his 1990 baptism that Deacon Mark Springer used the "We" formula. As a result, Hood was not a Christian, let alone a priest, because he could not be validly ordained a priest if he was not validly baptized.*

Hood's situation was quickly remedied on Aug. 9 with his baptism and on Aug. 17 with his ordination. But the archdiocese is trying to track down everyone baptized by Deacon Springer, who served in Detroit from 1986 to 1999. How many other priests and deacons around the country used "We" is unknown?

But since his ordination in 2017 was invalid, people who went to Hood's "Masses" did not really attend Mass and did not receive consecrated bread at Communion. It also means that his absolutions in the confessional were not sacramental. His confirmations and anointing of the sick were also invalid. When he performed these sacraments, he was not even a Christian, let alone a priest.

Thankfully, his baptisms were valid because a non-Christian can perform a valid baptism.

Some Examples of Possible Charges

As we can see from the above reading and examples a person can be charged with an irregularity and the sacrament is deemed invalid for numerous reasons.

A person can be charged with the following, and there may be more based on the denomination's Code of Canon Law.

1. Dispensation of the sacrament without consent of the recipient.
2. Dispensation of the sacrament as a heretic
3. Disrespectful dispensing or reception of the sacrament
4. Improper intent on the part of the dispenser of the sacrament
5. Improper form of the sacrament
6. Improper matter of the sacrament
7. Forcible dispensation of the sacrament by the minister
8. Acceptance of the sacrament with improper intent to receive.
9. Illicit and invalid sacramental dispensation by someone who is not a valid and licit minister.
10. Other illicit or invalid acts as described in ecclesiastical law of the church.

With the exception of necessity, it is traditionally illicit for anyone without permission to baptize outside their own territory (see Code of Canon Law, CLSA, 1983). In other words, unless a priest or anyone designated person able to perform a baptism according to that church's Canon Law (any church not just the Roman Catholic Church but any Independent movement catholic church), has permission from the Ordinary of the Diocese or Administrator in charge, if they perform the baptism it is illicit and has to be redone. There is, however, an issue with this statement. Some Codes of Canon Law, clearly state that even someone not baptized can baptize with proper intent and the correct Form and Matter. If this is the case then the Baptism is valid and licit, and nothing has to be done. The problem comes in with documentation. Any and all sacraments have to be documented with records secure in a designated area particular to the denomination.

Possible Reconciliations and Dispositions

To reconcile any issue surrounding the sacraments, consultation must take place between the Interjurisdictional Lawyer and the hierarchy of the church. This meeting must take place at that level and no other level. For example, if a cleric performs the act the pastor of the parish cannot dispense that action. It must be done by the Ordinary or Administrative authority. Consult with the Canons of the Particular Church for directions in this matter.

If, as in the case above regarding the actions of Fr. Matthew Hood, it is found that the individual dispensing any sacrament is not validly ordained and everyone with whom that alleged cleric dispensed a sacrament is invalid due to the illicit nature of his non-ordination status, that person needs to be stopped and if, as was the case of Hood, never baptized, must first be baptized and then, if all requirements for ordination academically have been completed, be confirmed, have their confession heard and given a just penance then receive Holy Communion and then be ordained since his first ordination was invalid due to him not even being baptized. In other words, if not baptized then no other sacrament holds validity in that person. Hood's ordination is not considered a *sub conditione* ordination because there is no question as to the validity of his ordination. He simply was not ordained validly or licitly.

As you can see from the example above, the remedy for this is to have all the sacraments conferred and then find all those who received sacraments from him and redo the sacraments.

If the Ordinary of the Diocese or denomination does not want to do the footwork to fix this ecclesiastical mess, it can be referred to the Interjurisdictional Canon Lawyer. If it goes to an Interjurisdictional Court, then any censures or sanctions made on the cleric are determined by the court, and the judge or justice makes the final decision, and the church needs to understand that the court's decision is final in this matter only and the disposition does not carry over to any other matter of this nature in the church. If the church Administrator does not agree to this, then the case cannot be heard in an Interjurisdictional Court on any level.

Appeals if Relevant.

Unless there has been a violation and or illicit act, for example, a non-Christian attempt to perform the sacrament, or an improper *Form* or *Matter* has been used, there should be no appeal required since any Christian who is baptized can baptize another. In fact, according to Reese (2020-09-15), in Religious News Services, "non-Christians can perform baptisms."

Caution, however, needs to be taken in the event that the baptism has been done, with the exception of an infant, with the person's consent. If a person is Canonically considered at the age of reason, usually age 7, and able to consent, without any mental or physical impediment, then baptism takes effect. If a person is baptized without consent, there may be room for appeals to be made. However, always look to the denomination's Code of Canon Law for exceptions to the rule.

The Sacrament of Confirmation

In some Orthodox Catholic Churches, all sacraments of initiation, Baptism, Confirmation, and Holy Eucharist are done at the same time, usually in infancy, and done by a priest in the context of a liturgy. This is very valid and very licit so long as it is done according to the Orthodox canons.

In the Roman Catholic Church and most other Catholic and Christian churches, Confirmation is done in adolescents or adulthood and only by a Bishop except in some cases, the bishop may appoint a priest to perform the sacrament.

In the adolescent and adulthood stages when the sacrament is dispensed, the individual is trained through the church either in their religious education in elementary school (if in the Catholic or Orthodox School System), or if in the Public School System or tradition of the denomination, in Sunday School by the local parish.

A Brief Definition of the Sacrament of Confirmation

The Sacrament of Confirmation makes the individual a fully-fledged member of that denominational Church. Theologically, it *"confirms"* and renews their baptism and baptismal promises and, as this writer was taught, *makes you a soldier of God* (illustrating the power of the sacrament and commitment one makes to the church and to God).

The rite of confirmation is performed by a bishop and only a bishop unless otherwise specified in the denomination's Code of Canon Law. There are exceptions in some churches. If there is a territory that cannot be accessed by a bishop for one reason or another, and it is impossible for the bishop to confer the sacrament, the Ordinary of the Diocese may in some denominations appoint a Validly Ordained Priest (never a Deacon) to perform the Confirmation. This only happens in rare cases and for only that time. The final exception is in the Roman Catholic Church if the Rite of Christian Initiation for Adults (RCIA) is taught and permissions are given the priest may confer all the Sacraments of Initiation (Baptism, Confirmation, and Holy Eucharist) at the same time, usually done at the Easter Vigil or Easter Day Mass.

The Rite is performed, and it involves the anointing on the forehead of the candidate with *Holy Chrism* and the laying on of hands, with the pronouncement, *"Be sealed with the gift of the Holy Spirit."* Confirmation is scripturally based on Acts

19:6. The only issue with this passage is that only adults are confirmed. There is no mention in the Bible that children or infants are confirmed. However, refer to the denominational canon laws for the parameters of who can and cannot receive the sacrament.

The Minister of the Sacrament of Confirmation

In the Catholic Church system (Roman, Orthodox, or Independent) the official minister of the sacrament is the Bishop and no other with one exception in some denominations, that is, if there is no bishop available or the Confirmation ceremony cannot be postponed until a bishop is ready, the Ordinary of the Diocese or the Presiding Bishop of the Denomination may delegate a one-time *faculty (permission)* to the parish priest, or religious superior to do that confirmation only that one time.

Periodically, what is known as a *special agent*, usually a *catechist* may validly confer the sacrament. For example, if there is a country where there is no bishop or a priest who can only come periodically, then permission may be granted by universal law to a well-trained catechist.

The Form and Matter of the Sacrament of Confirmation

The Sacrament of Confirmation is conferred on the candidate through the anointing on the forehead with Holy Chrism, the imposition of hands on the head of the candidate accompanied by the appropriate form as found in the liturgical documents of the denomination.

The *Form* consists of the liturgy and the words of consecration. The liturgy should be celebrated within the context of church liturgy, however, there are exceptions, though rare, where there may not be a church or the ability to perform a liturgy, but there is a bishop, and the sacrament can be conferred through the anointing and laying on of hands along with the words, *Receive the Holy Spirit"* or another approved Form by the denomination.

The *Matter* is the Holy Chrism which must be consecrated only by a Bishop and the descent of the Holy Spirit strengthening the soul of the one being confirmed. A priest cannot consecrate chrism for any reason. If there is no chrism at the parish because there is no bishop, it should be mailed to that location or delivered in another manner. There is no exception to this rule. No chrism, no sacrament of Confirmation even if a Bishop is present.

In the Eastern Churches, any priest can validly confer the sacrament on any Catholic. This includes Roman Catholics but only to those belonging to that priest's particular church and Catholics who meet the conditions of either being their subjects or of being lawfully baptized by them, or being in danger of death (CLSA, Code of Canon Law, 1983, Canon 926).

The Invalidity, or Illicitness Relevant to the Sacrament of Confirmation.

1. Everyone who is first Baptized is eligible to be confirmed. If one is not Baptized they cannot be confirmed. If they are, the

sacrament is not valid, and this is considered an invalid and illicit sacrament.
2. An unauthorized person confers the sacrament. Without authorization from the Ordinary or Presiding Bishop for anyone other than a Bishop to confer the sacrament if the sacrament is conferred this is invalid and illicit.
3. If a person is forced into being confirmed without their consent and free will this is an impediment to the sacrament and the Confirmation is illicit and invalid.
4. If the person to be Confirmed is not of sound mind and does not understand the gravity or meaning of the Sacrament, the sacrament is invalid and illicit.
5. If according to the denominations Code of Canon Law, the age of the confirmand does not meet the criteria, this constitutes an impediment to the sacrament. If a Bishop confers the sacrament and is not knowledgeable of the age of the candidate the Sacrament is valid but illicit.
6. Other issues of validity and liceity are to be found in the denomination's Code of Canon Law.

Charges

Some of the charges that can be placed upon individuals who confer the Sacrament of Confirmation are:

1. Invalidity of the Sacrament due to an irregular or impeded minister of the sacrament. Someone other than a Bishop or validly appointed substitute conferred the sacrament. In this case, the one conferring the Sacrament is not a Bishop and has not been duly appointed by the Administrative Hierarchy. If this is the case the Sacrament is both invalid and illicit. In this case, it may be proper to censure or take another action again the cleric performing the illicit sacrament. The remedy is that the person is re-Confirmed by the proper minister.
2. Improper *Form* as an invalidating factor. The Sacrament was not appropriately conferred because the *Form* or substitute according to the denomination's Canon Law was violated, not performed within liturgical standards and rite, or not used without permission from the Ordinary or Presiding Bishop. The Sacrament has to be redone.
3. No *Form* is an invalidating factor to negate the effect of the sacrament. There was no *Form* used. Even though there may have been appropriate *Matter*, the lack of proper *Form* according to the liturgical guidelines

invalidates the Sacrament. The sacrament is invalid and illicit and needs to be redone.
4. If Improper *Matter* was used during the conferring of the Sacrament. Regardless of the presence of a Bishop or designated minister, Holy Chrism must be used and nothing else unless culturally mandated and approved by the denomination as is found in that denomination's Canon Law. If the irregularity is due to improper *Matter* the Sacrament does not hold and is invalid and has been dispensed illicitly and invalidly if not performed by a Bishop.

If the laying on of hands and the Holy Spirit was not called upon and imparted in the way specified by the denomination's liturgical guidelines the Sacrament, does not take effect.
5. Any other issues that are outlined in the denominations Code of Canon Law that invalidates, irregularities, impediments, or deems the Sacrament illicit can be considered a matter for the Interjurisdictional Lawyer to consider.

Possible Reconciliations

If it has been discovered that the Sacrament of Confirmation was not properly conferred and is invalid and illicit, all those who were confirmed must be confirmed again, this time properly according to the rubrics and Canon Law of that denomination.

To reconcile any issue surrounding the sacraments consultation must take place between the Interjurisdictional Lawyer and the hierarchy of the church. This meeting must take place at that level and no other level. For example, if anyone other than a Bishop or legally designated priest or another administrative official of the church dispenses the sacrament without proper authority, that constitutes an illicit Sacrament because someone other than a Bishop attempted the sacrament and therefore, the Sacrament is invalid and must be redone.

If there is to be a reconciliation between the church and the violator then reconciliation must be done by the Ordinary or Administrative authority at the Hierarchical level of Office. Consult with the Canons of the Particular Church for directions in this matter. If it goes to an Interjurisdictional Court, then the judge or justice makes the final decision, and the church needs to understand that the court's decision is final in this matter only and the disposition does not carry over to any other matter of this nature in the church. If the church Administrator does not agree to this, then the case cannot be heard in an Interjurisdictional Court on any level. The lawyer may be used as a consultant in this matter to give advice, if needed, concerning the way to proceed to fix this issue justly.

Dispositions and Appeals if Relevant.

Any issues regarding the dispensing of or effect of the sacrament of Confirmation are left up to the Ordinary of the Diocese or Administrative Church Official up to and including the Presiding Bishop.

If a Confirmation is questionable, and the confirmand believes that he or she has been validly and licitly confirmed, the Interjurisdictional Canon Lawyer can represent a defendant if he or she believes they have been unjustly accused. The lawyer can also work with the plaintiff if issues arise, and the incident needs to stand before a court. Regardless of defense, if the sacrament was improperly performed or an irregularity to the sacrament has been considered and in fact, the person was not validly and licitly confirmed, that person has to redo the confirmation, or they are not confirmed.

In the rare case that improprieties on any level go beyond the Ordinary of the Diocese, the Chancery officer, or local administrative authorities handle the cases individually and effectively. In the best case, the person may just have to redo the Confirmation over.

The Sacrament of Reconciliation (Confession)

Definition of the Sacrament

The Sacrament of Reconciliation also known as Confession or Penance has its etiology dating back to the Old Testament (**Hebrew**: גיור,: [giyur] or שׁוּב: [Shub] To turn back or to return). The word *Reconciliation,* according to Scuderi (2022) in *A Text, Commentary and Canon Law of the Ecumenical Catholic Church of Christ-Worldwide* states that the term *Reconciliation* is meant to be a "healing re-joining of God to His Church to mend the break that humanity created from the story we read in Genesis of the first sin of Adam and Eve.

The name *Confession* discloses one's sins to a priest and "unloads" their sins (Scuderi, 2022, A Text, Commentary and Canon Law of the Ecumenical Catholic Church of Christ-Worldwide). Scuderi (2022) sees the reason for confessing one's sins to an Ordained Priest as essential in the administration, conferring, and conclusion of (absolution of the penitent) the sacrament. The priest, according to Scuderi (2022) acts "in place of Jesus the Christ as one who removes and forgives the sins of the penitent. This is not a symbolic gesture; this is a mystical event that actually happens. In the confessional or, wherever the penitent and priest meet, there Christ is really present. It is important for Catholics to confess their sins to a priest because, first, seek forgiveness the way Christ intended. Second, by confessing to a priest, the Catholic learns a lesson in humility, which Is avoided when one confesses only through private prayer," not to negate private prayer which is essential. This context is referencing the person who says they don't need a priest because they can go directly to God. Which holds merit on one level, but on another level, Jesus did say to Peter and the Apostles, to paraphrase, if someone confesses their sins and you lose those sins, they forgiven, but hold it bound and it is held bound. Jesus did not say, tell those who want to confess their sins to tell them directly to God and all will be well (See John 20:23). The third reason to go to a priest to hear one's confession is the sacramental grace the non-Catholic does not receive through the absolution process. Fourth, the Catholic is assured that his or her sins are forgiven, and they do not need to depend on subjective feelings, thoughts, or wondering if God heard them. Finally, the Catholic can also obtain sound advice on avoiding sin in the future (Retrieved from The Forgiveness of Sins on https:// www.catholic.com/tract/the-forgiveness-of-sins.)

The Sacrament takes effect with the words of the priest: *I absolve you of your sins, in the name of the Father, and of the Son, and of the Holy Spirit. Amen,* and this is followed by a penance which is usually a series of sincere prayers or an act that someone has to do to reconcile themselves with their neighbor or both.

The Minister of the Sacrament

The de facto minister of the Sacrament of Reconciliation in any Code of Canon Law is the priest and only the priest (this includes Bishops of course) and they must have valid faculties and jurisdiction. A safe and best example of the process of the Sacrament of Confession is found in the Roman Catholic Canons (967§3) which describes the Sacrament of Reconciliation as not only a sacrament but also a sacrament of jurisdiction for the priest. Therefore, to do confessions, the priest must be validly and licitly ordained and given the proper faculties in the jurisdiction to which he or she serves. A superior of a Religious Order may also be granted faculties to hear confession and these faculties, because of the missionary status of most religious orders, institutes, or societies of apostolic life, possess faculties everywhere by the law itself but only for those living in the religious house or monastery. These faculties are valid until a superior removes them. If that person of a Religious Order or institute or society of apostolic life goes outside their house and into a local parish, as their ministry, then outside the house they must be granted faculties to do confessions and all sacraments by the Ordinary of the Diocese or they act validly but illicitly. This, however, applies to the Roman Catholic Church and may be different in other denominations so before any decision is made to assess invalidity or illicitness, as always, check the denomination's canons and if not there ask an Administrator of the church or the Ordinary what that church's policy is on the dispensing of any and all sacraments. Never assume that one law fits all denominations. Each denomination though seems similar, there are different. If an occasion arises where a priest who does not have the faculties to hear confessions and pretends without good reason, for example in a dire emergency or death of a person requestion to have their confession heard, the sacrament is valid but illicit. In this case, the church should *supplant* (supply) the missing faculty leading to the validity of the sacrament (CLSA, 1983, Can.144). Again, this is a Canon from the Code of Canon Law of 1983 from the Roman Church. Though an excellent remedy for the resolution of invalidity, not all churches may have this policy. In that case, the Interjurisdictional Canon Lawyer may suggest a form of this canon be applied in this situation and added to their own canon law.

    A Deacon may never hear a confession, nor could a layperson. There is no such thing in Canon Law as someone being "appointed" to hear a confession.

    The Sacrament of Reconciliation and the reception and forgiveness of sins by a priest is sacrosanct! The priest is under *the seal of confession* which may never be broken even if the priest leaves the priesthood. The *seal of confession* is the grave and strict obligation never to reveal any information that would identify sin with a particular penitent. The absolute secrecy applies in ALL circumstances, whatsoever. There are no exceptions even under the penalty of incarceration. The rationale for this is due to the delicacy of confession and to maintain the honor of the sacrament. In the event that this deal is broken the priest or Bishop, if directly or indirectly violates this seal is immediately excommunicated with penalties to follow after death.

The ability to hear confessions comes from *faculties* (permission) given to the priest from the Local Ordinary where the priest is assigned. The exception is, for example, the ordained Franciscan Friar or missionary in any Order, who may have the privilege to hear confessions anywhere at any time even without the permission of the local ordinary as outlined above.

If a priest leaves the priesthood, in most Catholic churches, that priest cannot function as a priest, in case of a dire emergency, for example, someone is dying, or there is a disaster and there is no priest around or available, even though the faculties are revoked that former priest may validly and licitly hear confessions and absolve sins validly and licitly. " In urgent necessity, any confessor is obliged to hear the confessions of the Christian faithful, and in danger of death, any priest is so obliged" (CLSA Code of Canon Law, 1983, Canon 986 §2). However, this does not apply to all denominations. The Interjurisdictional

Lawyer must familiarize him or herself with the canons of the denomination they are defending or prosecuting for guidelines about confessional permissions.

The Form of the Sacrament of Reconciliation

The *Form* of the Sacrament of reconciliation are the words, *I absolve you of all your sins, in the name of the Father and of the Son and of the Holy Spirit. Amen.*

This Form may also be used: *May our Lord and God, Jesus Christ, through the grace and mercies of his love for humankind, forgive you all your transgressions. And I, an unworthy priest, by his power given me, forgive and absolve you from all your sins, in the name of the Father and of the Son and of the Holy Spirit. Amen.*

This *Form* is the most current *Form* used in the Roman Catholic Church:

God, the Father of mercies, through the death and resurrection of His Son has reconciled the world to Himself and sent the Holy Spirit among us for the forgiveness of sins; Through the ministry of the Church, may God give you pardon and peace, and I absolve you from your sins in the name of the Father, and of the Son, and of the Holy Spirit.

The Matter of the Sacrament of Reconciliation

The *Matter* in the Sacrament of Reconciliation is the sin that is confessed.

Charges and Appeals Regarding Illicit & Invalid Acts

Here are only a few issues that may arise where the Interjurisdictional Canon Lawyer may be requested to litigate. For any violations or issues needing litigation, as always, refer to that denomination's Code of Canon Law.

1. A non-ordained priest hears a confession. In this instance, the individual is *impersonating the clergy*. If that person is a member of a Church in the Interjurisdictional realm, that person is subject to an ecclesiastical hearing or brought to the Ordinary of the diocese for a disposition of this incident. The individual is eligible, as is anyone to representation by an Interjurisdictional lawyer. In cases like this one, the imposter may be censured and excommunicated from the church, or if deemed mentally challenged be remanded to psychotherapy with a review from the psychotherapist to be given to the Ordinary of the Diocese or appointed Administrator to decide the next step.

    Once treatment is received and the individual is medically cleared and found to be of a more appropriate mental status, that person will be brought before the Ordinary of the Diocese or Presiding Bishop to discuss the gravity of the situation. If that person is repentant and understands that he or she must never perform any sacrament, the sin is absolved, and the censure is lifted. The person may then enjoy the gifts of the sacrament.

    If that same person offends in a similar manner with this or any other sacrament, then, regardless of mental status, that person will be excommunicated or penalized according to the denomination's Code of Canon Law. This incident will be written and available for public review as a caution to other churches and depending on the Civil Laws, that individual may be charged with impersonating a priest.

Furthermore, the impersonator may be handed over to the Civil authorities for the crime of impersonating a clergyperson. Most societies do see any form of impersonation of authority as a Civil crime. Turning this individual over to the authorities is not breaching the seal of confession. It is meting out justice. If the penitent was under the belief that the person whom they told their confession to be a real priest, one of two things can happen depending on Church law. The first is that person's sins are forgiven, and it ends there the person does not have to confess their sins all over again and be retraumatized. The second thing is that person, without confessing all over again can receive a general absolution and it ends there. The final solution is that the person goes to a priest and retells the confession.

2. If a priest is forced to hear a confession and absolve the sin, but the priest does not have proper intent to absolve and believes that

the sin is bound, but absolved fearing for his or her life or has been put under undue influence or duress, this invalidates the sacrament and is illicit. The absolution does not take effect and the sin is held bound.

3. If the priest hears confession with improper intent and refuses to absolve the penitent's sins for reasons other than a legitimate reason for holding that person bound, this is illicit on the part of the priest. Depending on the Canons of the Church, this can lead to censuring the priest for a time, or some other penalty as outlined in the denomination's Code of Canon Law. If the priest is accused of this action but insists that the accusations are not true, that priest may enjoy the services of the Interjurisdictional Canon Lawyer who should first get a deposition from the priest and then request an audience with the ordinary of the diocese to discuss the matter to find a reconciliation point. If it is still believed that the priest was falsely accused the next step would be to take this to an Interjurisdictional Court and try the case. If it goes to court then all sides must understand that the court's decision is final pending an appeal. Regardless of what happens, due process under the law must take precedence.

4. Other impediments, improprieties, or irregularities are to be found in the

denomination's Code of Canon Law and are to be treated and adjudicated accordingly.

The main issue regarding the Sacrament of Reconciliation is the consideration of urgency in receiving the sacrament, and the proper minister officiating at and dispensing the sacrament.

Considering the urgency in receiving the Sacrament of Reconciliation, Canonically, in most Catholic denominations *ONLY* a priest or bishop may preside at the dispensation of the sacrament. In those exceptional cases a former priest who is no longer affiliated with the church, within certain criteria found in the church's canon laws, may also hear confessions in the event of a dire emergency or catastrophe where there is no other priest present. If it can be proven that there was an urgency the Sacrament holds, and no charges are established.

Any irregularities above discuss the issue of an individual who is an imposter, and not a priest, or a priest that has been censured or has had their orders suspended for cause, then, if that individual is church-affiliated, they can be charged with the illegal dispensing of a sacrament subject to the denomination's Canon Laws and may use the services of an Interjurisdictional Canon Lawyer to assist.

Possible Reconciliations

Depending on the mental status of the defendant, reconciliation can be as simple as an acknowledgment of the action, true confession, and absolution and it ends there.

If it is a censured or otherwise disciplined person of the clergy, it can mean the removal of Holy Orders, secularization, or laicization up to, and including, excommunication.

Always confer with the church's Code of Canon Law for any directions for dealing with people who are committing sacramental improprieties.

The Sacrament of the Holy Eucharist

The Sacrament of the Holy Eucharist must be understood by the Interjurisdictional Canon Lawyer for each denomination. Though every Catholic Church believes that the bread and wine mystically change into the real presence of Jesus Christ review the canons of the church and the Theology of the church to understand exactly when the mystagogical transformation actually transubstantiates. Also, take note of what elements are used to confect the Blessed Sacrament, and what happens to the elements after the celebration of mass is over, and there is consecrated bread and wine left. For example, the bread that is used can determine the validity or liceity of the Sacrament. The Eastern Church, for example, uses leavened wheaten bread for the Eucharist, whereas the Latin Rite Church (Roman Catholic and other Independent Catholic Churches using the Latin model) use unleavened bread (hosts). Certain Eastern Rite Churches use rice or rye flour or honey, butter, or eggs. If the wrong *Matter* is used then it is believed that transubstantiation does not occur and that invalidates the entire Liturgy or Mass.

Here is a scenario for you to think about from this writer's seminary days back in the 1980s. During that period in history, the Roman Catholic Church was going through tumultuous times. Women were insisting they wanted to be ordained priests. Some formed their own groups and started saying mass. Priests were leaving to get married. Churches were merging due to low parishioner attendance and the seminary liturgy class talked about and handed out recipes (which I still have) on how to make communion bread using, honey, flower, water, and other ingredients. The bread never really rose, but in some cases it did, and it also never had the look of a host, and it was very chewy. We made the bread and those who were ordained, usually the professors and occasionally a newly ordained graduate, used it at mass. The question for the reader is this: Was this a valid and licit mass or was the entire mass invalid and therefore illicit? Remember, a real ordained priest celebrated mass. Regardless of the celebrant's status was this liturgy valid and licit? If so, what made it valid and licit? If not, was the mass valid and illicit? If so, what made it valid and illicit? Was the mass invalid yet licit? If so, what invalidated the mass, and what made it licit? Was the mass illicit and therefore invalid? What was the cause of this?

What occurs if the priest uses an invalid wine by canon law? Some churches, in special circumstances, for example, an alcoholic priest, through the authority of the Ordinary of the Diocese, and sometimes the Canon Laws, allow for the use of Grape Juice, but the valid Matter, wine, is one made of grapes that is fermented and is "real" wine that is not mixed with any other substance other than water could make the wine invalid. However, given the process of winemaking and the many different factors that can make wine go bad, the use of chemicals is part of the inorganic process of winemaking. However, some specialty church wines, which can be quite expensive, are organic in nature and there is no question as to its validity during Mass.

The *Sacrament of the Holy Eucharist* is also called *Holy Communion*. This is the main sacrament of the Catholic Church. The Rite of Holy Communion in the liturgy is a reenactment of the Last Supper where Jesus mystically changed bread into his body and wine into his blood. This is not conjecture nor is it meant to be defined as a memorial. During the Last Supper, Jesus de facto imparted on the Apostles the ability to confect the Blessed Sacrament and to pass that power down to all ordained priests and bishops. Therefore, when a priest or bishop, at the liturgy says the words of consecration, the bread turns into the real flesh and the wine turns into the real blood of Christ under the guise of bread and wine. This is called *transubstantiation*. It should be noted that this action and event is by no means a form of cannibalism. The true essence of Jesus is present in the sacrament and as we eat the body and drink the blood we are receiving mystically, and actually the real presence of God within us. God truly dwells within us. God is in us. This is why we must approach this sacrament with a pure heart and mind, or we are guilty of disrespectfully receiving the body and blood of Christ.

Only a priest may confect the Blessed Sacrament. A Deacon may not. However, the distribution of the Blessed Sacrament may be done by any validly ordained minister including what the Roman Catholic and other Catholic denominational Churches call, *extraordinary ministers of the Eucharist.*

In the absence of a priest at Sunday Liturgy, A Deacon or Lay minister (extraordinary minister of the Eucharist) may have a *liturgical prayer service* in place of Sunday mass, but in order for the faithful to receive the Holy Eucharist validly and licitly, there must be enough of the Blesses Sacrament reserved that has been consecrated beforehand by a priest or bishop. Under no circumstances can the power of the priesthood be "temporally" given to a Deacon or anyone else. Only a priest or bishop, as mentioned above, has the right and privilege to consecrate the Holy Eucharist.

The Form of the Sacrament of Holy Communion

During the Mass, there is the Rite of Communion which involves the *Epiclesis* followed by the consecratory prayer. During the *Epiclesis* the priest or bishop invokes the Holy Spirit and says the following (depending on the tradition of the Catholic Church. The Orthodox Catholics for example have a different formula. Nonetheless, both change mere bread and wine into the real presence of Jesus), and then say the consecratory prayer:

On the night he was betrayed he took bread, said the blessing, broke the bread, and gave it to his disciples saying, 'take this all of you and eat it for this is my body.

When supper was ended, he took the chalice filled with wine. He said the blessing and gave the chalice to his disciples and said, 'take this all of you and drink for it, for this is the chalice of my blood, the blood of the new and everlasting covenant. Whenever you do this, remember me (some write: 'do this in remembrance of me').

The Matter of the Sacrament of Holy Communion

As explained above, the Matter of the Sacrament of Holy Communion is simply unleavened bread for some Catholic Denominations, or leavened bread for the Orthodox Church and other denominations, and wine.

Illicit and Invalidating Acts

For many years there have been issues in all churches of all faiths concerning the alcoholic priest and parishioners. At one point in the church's history, it did not matter if anyone had this issue with the consumption of alcohol or not, it must be wine. This tradition of bread and wine during liturgy stems back to the Last Supper. However, for some denominations, with a special *dispensation* from the Ordinary of the Diocese or by mandate of the Presiding Bishop or by Canon Law, the use of grape juice (non-alcoholic) may be used. However, the preference is wine (as was mentioned earlier above).

In all these examples the Interjurisdictional Canon Lawyer may be called upon to litigate if deemed by the involved Church that a situation is serious enough to be litigated, or the lawyer may act as a mediator between the defendant, or plaintiff, and the Church.

1. If a person poses as a priest, for example, a seminarian on an internship that practices the mass and invites parishioners to join him or her, and does not tell them that he is practicing saying mass, and knowingly and willingly or even by mere action of confecting the Blessed Sacrament performs the ritual and distributes bread and wine in the guise of real presence, this constitutes both an irregularity to Holy Orders and an Impediment to Holy Orders, not to mention fraud and impersonating an ordained minister. This seminarian can be dismissed immediately for such actions. Any form of appeal at this level is up to the Diocese or Order. An Interjurisdictional Canon Lawyer can represent the seminarian, but usually, any actions to remove the seminarian are left to those who have been involved with his training.

2. If a Deacon holds a liturgy and simply not a Communion Service and attempts to confect the Blessed Sacrament, that Deacon can be censured, removed, secularized, or laicized, or any other penalty as presented in the denominations Code of Canon Law. This action is illicit therefore invalidating the entire liturgy.

3. If any member of the clergy or anyone desecrates the Blessed Sacrament, constituting a sin against the Blessed Sacrament that person is excommunicated. Any other penalties should be presented in the denomination's Code of Canon Law. If a person feels they have unjustly

been charged with this, they may assume the services of an Interjurisdictional Canon Lawyer who may take a deposition and possibly decide to defend this case. It is up to the church to challenge the defense and hire an Interjurisdictional Canon Lawyer to prosecute this case in court. The preponderance of evidence lies on the plaintiff to prove the guilt beyond a reasonable doubt.

4. Other censures, punishments, and penalties should be found in the denomination's Code of Canon law along with the processes and procedures to determine guilt or innocence.

5. In Catholic Churches where a priest who has been laicized, suspended, or excommunicated is not to celebrate the Liturgy of the Eucharist, but if the Mass is said, the consecration and the mass are valid but illicit.

Possible Reconciliations for Violations Against the Sacrament of the Holy Eucharist

If it has been decided either by the administrative clergy, Presiding Bishop, or Interjurisdictional Ecclesiastical Court that the violation was inadvertent, a non-egregious act, or an unavoidable act or event, short of desecration of the Blessed Sacrament, can be handled on the parochial level through the Sacrament of Reconciliation.

If, however, the act was deemed egregious with malice and forethought, violence to the Blessed

Sacrament in any manner immediate excommunication without a chance for reconciliation may take place. This is the decision of the Ordinary of the Diocese or the Presiding Bishop who has the privilege to do with that person what they see is right and just.

If the chief Administrator has not decided the outcome of the case, and, after a period of 5 years has passed and no other incidents have been reported, the individual may petition the Church for reinstatement into the Church and congregation. If this is the case, the individual first must be absolved from the sin through the sacrament of reconciliation. Next, that person must meet with the Ordinary of the Diocese or the Presiding Bishop who will interview the person and determine if reconciliation is possible. If it is possible the Bishop will give directions on what he or she wants to be done to reinstate the individual, or not accept that individual back into the church. At that time, if the individual is not accepted, they may employ the services of the Interjurisdictional Canon Lawyer to appeal the decision in an Ecclesial Court. The burden of proof must be presented by the plaintiff and proven to be true and factual, or the case is dismissed, and the person has the right to be reinstated. If it does go to the courtroom level, the final disposition of the court can be appealed if unfavorable. However, whatever decision is made at that time, whether for the judge to hear the case or have the judge let the original verdict stand or be dismissed is the final decision and must be accepted by both parties without prejudice and retaliation.

Dispositions and Appeals

For any violation of the Holy Eucharist, the church authority makes the first call on what happens to the offender. If the church official decides that the act is egregious enough to demand excommunication then the person is immediately excommunicated. However, if the person feels they have been unjustly treated by the Church (the Administrative Authority), then the person may employ the services of the Interjurisdictional Canon Lawyer who would take the necessary depositions and file a case in Ecclesial Court. The Court will decide based on the Amicus Curé brief presented to the court if it will take the case or not. If the case is taken, a trial will occur. If there is a trial, the defendant must prove beyond a reasonable doubt that they are innocent. If proven, the church must reinstate the person and welcome that person back to the church. However, the church may require, if it wishes, that person does a formal confession of sins and penance attached. If the defendant agrees the reinstatement occurs, if the defendant refuses the church has the right not to accept the person back into the fold and the case is over with no chance of appeal.

Always refer to the denominational Code of Canon Law for the church's rules on the desecration of the Blessed Sacrament.

The Sacrament of Anointing of the Sick

Definition of the Sacrament of the Anointing of the Sick

Every priest has the privilege to administer the Sacrament of the Anointing of the Sick validly. It is given to the priest because the priest is entrusted with the spiritual care of his or her parishioners. With permission from the parish priest, priests outside that particular parish may also celebrate this Sacrament.

This sacrament used to be called, and in some Old Catholic Churches is still called, *Extreme Unction* or *Last Rites*. At one point in Church history, this sacrament was dispensed to those on their death bed. In modern times, this Sacrament is dispensed to anyone in need of healing. Churches even use this sacrament communally in anointing church services for those who may be ill or dealing with personal issues or even those with a terminal illness that may still be ambulatory or have mental challenges.

The Form of the Sacrament of Anointing of the Sick

The oil used in the Anointing of the Sick is blessed only by a Bishop and distributed by the bishop to his or her clergy. The form used in the blessing of the oil is found in the Holy Thursday Chrism Mass. The form for the actual anointing can be found in each denomination's sacramental texts where blessings and anointings are located. In some denominations, this is called the *Sacramentary*. Though some clergy may make up their own Form when anointing or dispensing a sacrament, the proper practice is to use the approved formula from each denomination's rubrics and according to their laws.

The anointings are to be carried out accurately using the words from the denomination's rite of anointing. In some instances, there are multiple anointings, on the forehead, eyes, nose, lips, ears, and breast near the heart. However, one simple anointing on the forehead is sufficient to have the sacrament dispensed appropriately.

Anointings are done by the person dispensing the sacrament, who is a cleric. A layperson may read the anointing ritual while the cleric anoints, in some faith traditions. Laypeople in some instances Interjurisdictional venues might be able to assist in the anointing, however, this practice is discouraged. Since it is a sacrament, the appropriate minister should dispense with the sacrament and that is a member of the Ordained clergy.

Those charged with the care of souls, the priest, is the proper minister of this sacrament with the obligation to administer the sacrament in their time of need.

Public anointings are permitted in an appropriate liturgical anointing service, or within the context of the Mass in a part of the liturgy that affords itself the space for the anointings.

The oils may be carried in a suitable bottle with a secure lid, or another suitable vessel by the priest anytime in the event that the need for its use occurs.

Generally, this sacrament is dispensed to the sick and dying. The word, *sick* in this context does not necessarily only mean physical illness. *Sickness* can range from the uncomfortable troubling thought or feeling to mental distress or a compromised mental status, or, as it was initially intended, given to those in dire need facing death.

The Matter of the Sacrament of the Anointing of the Sick

Oleum Infirmorum ('oil of the sick'), blessed by a Bishop is the only Holy Oil that should be used to dispense the Sacrament.

Illicit and Invalid uses of the Sacrament of the Anointing of the Sick

1. Oil that has not been properly blessed, or not blessed at all can be considered an *illicit act* of the sacrament because of the violation of the rubrics. The whole point of the sacrament is one of healing. The healing powers of the sacrament come from the ritualistic calling down of the Holy Spirit on the oil. This *illicit* action also invalidates the sacrament and therefore the sacrament has no effect.

2. The wrong Oil may lead to an irregularity. The oil to be used is Olive Oil. If Canola, Sunflower Seed Oil, or any oil other than Olive Oil is used that constitutes the irregularity and though valid, if done by a priest, it is illicit.

3. If a minister other than a priest dispenses the sacrament unless the Canons of the church say otherwise, this action is illicit and invalid.

4. Lack of, improper, or inappropriate Form is an impediment to the Sacrament because it blocks the effect of the sacrament and the meaning of the sacrament. Therefore, the sacrament is invalid. It also nullifies the ritual meaning of the sacrament. Every sacrament has a ritual attached to it. The words have tremendous meaning. One should never assume that any words are within reason to use. If a priest performs the sacrament it most probably is licit but remains invalid.

5. Inappropriate use of the Holy Oils is a sinful act. The Holy Oils are traditional in nature and blessed specifically for the purpose of anointing the sick and those dying. Any other inappropriate use, such as cooking with the oil, or giving a massage using the oils is a sinful act and must cease. This irresponsible use can lead to censure or excommunication if special circumstances are not the cause.

6. Other acts of invalidity or illicit use of the sacrament should be found in the denomination's Code of Canon Law.

Possible Reconciliations for Violations against the Sacrament of the Anointing of the Sick

Desecration of the Holy Oils is a sinful action. This sin can be easily remitted through the sacrament of reconciliation with sincere contrition and penance. In the event that the denomination, chooses a more severe punishment, such as censure or excommunication, this should be investigated by the Interjurisdictional Canon Lawyer through a study of the denomination's Canon Law and then through deposition from the accuser investigating the cause of the action, followed by either a petition by the lawyer to remove the censure or excommunication by the administrative authority of the church or litigate in an Ecclesiastical Interjurisdictional Court. If it goes to litigation, both sides must agree that the decision of the court is final, and the denomination must abide by the court decision. If the denomination does not agree, the case cannot be heard and, unfortunately, the admonition by the plaintiff must stand. However, if the administrative authority is on the diocesan or archdiocesan level, a brief should be prepared by the defense and the Interjurisdictional Canon Lawyer should appeal to the Ordinary of the diocese. If the accusations have not been made by the Ordinary, or if they have, then an appeal should be made to the Presiding Bishop who may choose to dispose of the case with *prejudice*, meaning that whatever charges were litigated will stand, or *without prejudice* where the Presiding Bishop will either hear the case him or herself or order the case to be brought before the Supreme Ecclesiastical Court (in some churches called the Tribunal Court). If it is brought to that level, it is understood that whatever the outcome, that decision is final and cannot be appealed. Always look to the denominations Code of Canon Law for any type of guidance for any case where there may be a question.

Dispositions and Appeals

As mentioned above if reconciliation is not ascertained through a good confession (a sincere, remorseful confession of sins with an appropriate penance), then the next step is to present an *amicus brief* to the court to hear the case and, if accepted to be heard, then a subpoena is presented to both the defendant and the plaintiff who will have a hearing. The defendant and plaintiff may seek depositions and bring in witnesses for presentation as the case stands trial. If at the first level of trial the case does not fall on the side of the defendant, the Interjurisdictional Canon Lawyer may petition for an appeal at the appellant level of the court system or petition the appointed denominational administrator, through the presentation of evidence by way of an amicus brief to consider a lesser charge or removal of the charges. If that disposition does not fall in favor of the defendant the Interjurisdictional Lawyer may petition the Supreme Interjurisdictional Court to hear the case. If it goes to that level, a retrial of the case occurs and all witnesses, and new ones if found, are heard. Any and all hierarchy or administrators appointed by the denomination may both, be present at the hearing as observers or may present their witnesses or be a witness themselves to testify in the adjudication of the case. Whatever happens, if it gets to this level both parties must agree before the hearing that the justices' decision is final and binding. This is a one-time disposition. If the person commits the same crime, all new evidence must be brought forward and the only thing that can be asked, if the court will allow it, is the question, *"have you ever been convicted, censured for, or previously had an excommunication reversed on a similar charge."* Regardless of the answer, no evidence from the previous case is to be brought into the trial this is called *double jeopardy* and the trial is considered a mistrial and must be retried or dismissed with an admonishment for both prosecution and defense. If a retrial happens and the evidence that has been suppressed from a previous trial has been brought into evidence, a mistrial is called, the case is dropped as are all charges, and the defendant may assume his or her position in the church.

If the denomination's Code of Canon Law specifies a particular disposition clearly stated in the law, that law is followed and there would be no need for any litigation unless the accused can prove that fabrication of the evidence or prejudice on the part of the plaintiff has occurred.

Chapter 3

Irregularities and Impediments

The Sacraments of Holy Orders (Deaconate, Presbyterate, Episcopacy) and Matrimony

Impediments or Irregularities

We begin our discussion with the definitions of an Impediment and Irregularity.

An *Impediment* is a hindrance or obstruction in the performance of a task. It makes it impossible to move forward. It slows and can block the progress of meeting a final requirement. In Roman Canon Law (1993), an Impediment is **a legal obstacle that prevents a sacrament from being performed either validly or licitly or both.** The term is used most frequently in relation to the sacraments of Marriage and Holy Orders.

Referring again to Canon 1041 of the Roman Code of Canon Law (1983), An *irregularity* is **a canonical impediment directly impeding the reception of tonsure and holy orders or preventing the exercise of orders already received**. Mental illness that prevents the fulfillment of the duties of the priesthood. Physical incapacity to perform the rites of the Church is a few examples of impediments.

Even though these definitions are derived from Roman Canon Law, they are quite relevant in Interjurisdictional Canon Law. A review of several denominational canons does not really define or call issues relevant to marriage and priesthood ordination impediments or irregularities. It is of little consequence to name the faith-based communities whose canons do not address by these titles issues that may arise in two people getting married or ordained. However, it is important that the Interjurisdictional Canon Lawyer has a springboard or keystone point from which to address any issues that may arise when defending or prosecuting a case. Therefore, for all intense and purposes, the above definitions will be used and explained below to assist in the adjudication of diverse cases that have issues related to marriage and Holy Orders.

Impediments

As a legal obstacle that will prevent a person from receiving a sacrament or performing a sacrament validly or licitly or both, an impediment is a word that is used in relation to the sacrament of Matrimony or Holy Orders. It should be noted that traditionally, some impediments can be removed whereas others remain for all time. When looking at diverse church Codes of Canon Law, see and understand which "impediments" may be removed, how they are removed, and who can remove them. Also, note the status of the individual and the ability to receive or not receive a sacrament after the removal of the impediment. In some instances, the impediment may be removed, but the person may still be ineligible to receive the sacrament. Actually, this makes no logical sense. If an impediment is removed, that means that the issue is resolved as if it did not happen, or it is forgiven. When a sin, for example, is forgiven, it is over, and the person is not bound to the issues surrounding that sin. Remember, what Jesus said to

Peter? The account of Jesus' first appearance in the Gospel of John (20:19-23; 21:13) shows similarity to the account in the Gospel of Luke (24:36–49), that it happened in Jerusalem on the evening of his resurrection from the dead (Guthrie, 1994).

Jesus' promise here is given to the whole group of disciples (the verb is plural) (Kieffer, 2007), parallel to the promise in Matthew 16:19; Matthew 18:18 (Coogan, 2007). The disciples' power to forgive sins is linked to the gift of the Spirit in John 20:22, and not to human power (Coogan, 2007) The verbs for forgiving and retaining are in the passive form, indicating that God is the one in action (Coogan, 2007).

With the statement in this verse, Jesus declares that in his messianic community (the "new covenant") his followers ("Christians") now hold the key to membership, in contrast to the authority held by the Jewish leadership (represented by the Sanhedrin and the Pharisees at that time) to affirm or deny acceptance in the synagogues (the "old covenant") (Köstenberger, 2004).

John 20:23 is seen as the origin for the practice of Confession and Absolution by the Catholic, Lutheran, Eastern Orthodox, Oriental Orthodox, Assyrian Church of the East and Irvingian Churches, and the Anglican Communion.

These Christian denominations teach that the Church has been given the apostolic power to forgive sins (Hahn & Scott, 2008, and, Young, 1996).

If an impediment does occur it needs to be looked at in severity and consequence. Some impediments can easily be resolved by the local Diocesan authority whereas others may need to go to the denomination's Primatial or Holy See and be resolved at that level.

The Sacrament of Holy Matrimony (Marriage)

Within the Church, the minister of Holy Matrimony is either the Priest or Deacon (in some denominations, it may only be the priest. Check the canons on this issue). Depending in Civil society, the minister of matrimony, not seen as a sacrament, may be performed by a Justice of the Peace, Judge, and in some cases anyone with whom the bride and groom wish to have as their officiant (a friend, neighbor, relative etc. who is usually 18 years of age or older).

Traditionally, marriage has been defined as the union between a man and a woman. Any union contracted by two people must be done freely and without coercion. According to Catholic tradition, they must be baptized and unmarried adults. To be licit in the eyes of the Church, marriage must be witnessed by a priest or deacon. However, other provisions may be made within the canons of the church.

There is an issue within the realm of marriage and contracts. In modern times tradition is replaced with reality. Civil law states that anyone may be married so long as it is done freely, and without coercion, and the two are adults. This includes homosexual unions. A church may not allow homosexual unions, but the States do. At this point in time, it has been deemed Constitutional by the United States Supreme Court that men may marry men and women may marry women. However, some churches do not allow this, which is their right. In some churches if two men or two women want to get married they are excommunicated from the church. This is allowable and the right of the church in the United States of America. A church does not have to accept homosexual marriage; it is perfectly legal. However, if the State marries two men or two women, so long as the law states it is legal, they are a married couple validly and licitly, in the eyes of the State and nation. However, in a church that does not allow gay or lesbian unions, the marriage is viewed ecclesiastically as invalid and illicit, but civilly valid and licit. Therefore, even though the church may not recognize the union, that couple is married. If a couple comes to the Interjurisdictional Canon Lawyer to file a suit against the church for prejudice or a crime against the Constitution of the United States the lawyer needs to remind the couple about the separation of church and state and no matter how far they argue the case, it is a moot point and if they are not happy with their denomination that does not accept their union, they should seek a denomination that does and go there. In these churches, a marriage between two men or two women is an impediment to marital validity.

There is a difference between the actions showing validity and the action being licit. Validity implies *integrity* and liceity implies *legality*. An illustration of this is the Interjurisdictional Lawyer who goes into a civil courtroom and tries a divorce case and wins. Once discovered that the Interjurisdictional Lawyer is not a JD (Civil Attorney) the case is not overturned but the Interjurisdictional Lawyer is subject to sanctions by the court. Another analogy that can be used as an example is the laicized or defrocked priest or suspended priest who celebrates a wedding within the context of mass. Though the wedding is illicit, it is valid, and the couple is married in the eyes of the State.

Looking again to give terms to diverse types of impediments we go to the Code of Canon Law of 1983 of the Roman Catholic Church. Remember, these definitions may not apply to the church you may be representing, but the definitions of these impediments may be helpful in the defense or prosecution of your case.

Impediments Defined

The Diriment Impediment

The first thing we must do is understand the effect an impediment has on the sacrament of marriage. There is a difference between a *diriment* and an *impediment* regarding the effect on the sacrament.

A *diriment* is an impediment. It invalidates an attempted marriage. If something occurs that may **prohibit** the marriage, this is called an *impediment* making the marriage illicit but valid.

Diriment is derived from the Latin word, *dirimens* meaning "separating". That means the couple cannot be joined (Church of the Holy Cross, Dover, DE. Retrieved: 5/27/2022). This goes back to the Roman CIC of 1917 which saw marriage issues in two ways. The first was an *impediment* that rendered a marriage valid but not licit, and there was the *diriment* rendering the marriage invalid.

If there is a question concerning if a union cannot be made do a diriment impediment look to the Canons of that church. If they list prohibitive impediments leading to a diriment impediment and the individuals fall into this category, then there is an impediment, and the couple, at least on an ecclesiological level, cannot be married, but this may have no effect Civilly. If there are no listings in the Canons regarding impediments, go to the Ordinary of the Diocese or Presiding Bishop concerning the policy of the church and follow that rule. Just make sure what the prelate says you have in writing just in case issues arise from what the presiding bishop said.

In general, impediments are directly related to "a" person. An illustration of this may be that the person wishing to be married is already married and does not have a divorce decree and tells no one that he or she is already married. It is rare that a diriment impediment arises. There are usually other issues that arise that are handled in other canonical venues such as a priest in a celibate clergy faith tradition attempting marriage while still a functioning priest.

Marriage legislation in the civil realm includes impediments that are founded on moral or physical grounds. In these cases, society views marriages of this nature as detrimental to the couple, possible children, or the community. Examples may be incestuous marriages. For the more conservative churches, this may go into inter-religious marriages and marriages after divorce.

Historically marriage has been a means of propagation of the species, and for the good of communities throughout the world. As a form of control of the population and for some extremely racist and bigoted reasons to control the race, marriage has been subject to legal rules and regulations that include impediments that are based on moral and/or physical circumstances that societies have determined to be a hindrance to their existence as a society, political party, children, or the community at large.

Turning to Scripture, the Pauline Epistles address the issue of marriage and restrictions placed on marriages and household affairs as is seen in 1 Corinthians 5:1-5 where Paul addresses the issue of incest, marriage in 7:1-16, 25-40, slavery in 7:21-24, eating habits in 8:1-13;11:17-34 and finances in 16:1-4. Prohibitions on marriage in Paul include incestuous marriages, marriages with non-believers, and second marriages after divorce. In Roman Catholic Church history apostolic synods and councils "regularly passed legislation concerning marriage impediments. Much of this legislation was in response to community needs of abuses (CLSA, Canon Law, A Text, and Commentary, 1985).

The issue of divorce was addressed to the Corinthians. In 1 Cor. 4:14 he claims authority over the matter of divorce. He calls himself the father of that community and when addressing the Corinthian community, he calls them τέκνα μου; v.14 (my children) saying that he fathered or "begot" the community (ἐγὼ ὑμᾶς ἐγέννησα; v.14). This establishes him as the *paterfamilias* or *head of the household* (Ehrensperger, 2009). Since Paul claims to be head of the household, if anyone was to be divorced they had to go through him first. Ehrensperger (2009), talks about unbelievers marrying believers and the conflict that it will bring to the household. She alludes to the unbeliever converting to the Christian faith and then the unbeliever "would be sanctified" and "could amount to an approval of their ties to his [Paul's] household". However, if the unbeliever is not willing to accept Christianity then divorce was allowed so that ties between the unbeliever's household and the Christian household would cease. In canonical terms today this is called, *disparity of cult* and is grounds for an annulment in the Roman Catholic Church.

There are two types of impediments found in Canon Law literature. The first is called *divine law (that which comes from God)* and the second is called *ecclesiastical law (that which comes from the church or man)*.

The impediments associated with Divine law see marriage as a natural institution affecting all people regardless of baptismal status. Those impediments affiliated with ecclesiastical law find their basis in the sacramental nature of marriage in relation to the community of believers. Therefore, when discussing impediments with a church official and the couple when looking at annulments, understand where divine law begins and ends and where ecclesiastical law begins and ends. If the church you are dealing with has Synodical Councils understand that they regularly pass legislation regarding what constitutes an impediment to marriage and the course of action to be taken.

As a natural institution, meaning, this is what people do on a regular basis, marriage is based on Divine Law. With Divine law comes *Divine Law Impediments* which base marriage as a natural institution affecting everyone. The question in determining Divine Law Impediments is, Is this marriage good for society or not? If not, what makes it bad for society, and what is the remedy? *Ecclesiastical Law Impediments* have their basis in marriage as a sacrament and how that sacrament relates in the bigger picture to society and the community of believers.

When discussing Divine Law Impediments, canonical commentators agree that "the divine law impediments include prior bond, impotence, and consanguinity in the direct line (First-degree direct line includes: the individual's parents, siblings, and children) and in the second degree of the collateral line (relatives include: an individual's grandparents, grandchildren, uncles, aunts, nephews, and half-siblings). However, certain commentators view disparity of cult, sacred orders, and perpetual vows of chastity as divine law impediments" (CLSA, Canon Law: A Text and Commentary, 1993 and 1985). In dealing with cases where Divine Law Impediments are concerned, consult the denominations Code of Canon Law and the Presiding Bishop or Administrator in charge of ministering and interpreting the law of that church. They are the competent authority in such matters for their particular church.

The term, *Absolute Impediment*, is meant to affect all people regardless of baptismal status. When assessing an issue related to marriage look at how the impediment affects not only the couple but society and the church. If it is an impediment that seriously affects the couple, society and the church consider it an *Absolute Impediment*, whereas the term *Relative Impediment* applies to marriages in certain instances that may not affect the community or church, but only the couple seeking understanding in any realm. there are impediments known as *Perpetual Impediments*. These are very difficult impediments because they come with issues that usually are unresolvable and always remain. The last is the *Temporary Impediments*. These are the least severe of the Impediments and tend to go away over time through reconciliation or removal by the Ecclesiastical Authority.

Impediments are based on law. As such, if the law changes, an impediment, and definition thereof can change or be abolished. In canonical terms, the abolition of an impediment is called a *dispensation*. Only a competent ecclesiastical authority can dispense an impediment. The competent authority is defined in the denomination's Code of Canon Law but is usually the bishop of the diocese or the Presiding Bishop of the denomination. Therefore, in some cases, if the Ecclesiastical authority says that a person with an impediment can get married, that person can be validly and licitly married. This type of pronouncement is done on an individual basis. The authority may dispense the impediment on one person and hold the same impediment on another person.

Impediments can also go away with time, based on the circumstance of the impediment. If a person is divorced and re-married, and their church says there is an impediment because of the divorce and one of the couples dies, the impediment goes away. In less drastic situations, the couple may come up with a viable solution to dispense with the impediment and have it agreed upon by the church. To illustrate this think of the culture where a 12-year-old is allowed to marry. The family arranges the wedding and the boy and girl get married. They have sex and she gets pregnant, and they have the baby. This is called, *ratum et consummatum* (The marriage is ratified when it is consummated). The girl really didn't want to get married but because it was arranged she had to get married. If she really did not want to get married, then the marriage is invalid yet licit. The impediment would be an ecclesiastical impediment unless the marriage happened between consanguinity in the direct line and in the second degree of the collateral line,(grandparents, grandchildren, uncles, aunts, nephews, nieces, and half-siblings) as noted above.

Impediments in the Public Forum

Consanguinity and Affinity

One of the reasons it is important for the Interjurisdictional Canon Lawyer to understand the Civil laws governing marriage are the instances when an impediment concerns both Church and State. To illustrate this, consider Fred and Freda. Fred was married to Juliana for 5-years. It was a tumultuous relationship. Fred walked out on Juliana 2-years ago. They have not had any contact since Fred left. Fred met Freda at one of his family reunions. Freda is the stepsister of his cousin Mark, but Fred did not know this. He was introduced to her and shortly thereafter fell in love, and it was said to be "a match made in heaven." Fred proposes to Freda and Freda says, "yes".

This case has a plethora of canonical issues. First, this relationship is an impeded relationship in the *public* realm. The existence of this relationship can be proven to be real in the public forum. All Mark has to do is tell Fred that Freda is his stepsister. At that point, if Fred understands the issue, he will not marry. If it is discovered by the officiant then the officiant should refuse to marry them. If the county does its due diligence, Fred and Freda should never have been granted the license to marry in the first place.

If it was rumored that Freda was the stepsister but could not be proven to be the step-sister, this would be considered an impediment in the *occult* realm since she may be a step-sister, but it is not certain nor provable in the public forum that she, in fact, is the stepsister. Whether this relationship is public, or occult is important especially if the church the Interjurisdictional Canon Lawyer is working with has rules about relationships of such nature. If a person is unaware of a blood relative then the impediment still exists and in some jurisdictions, the marriage is and should be, invalid, whereas, in other jurisdictions, it may not be viewed as an impediment. Look to the Code of Canon Law for direction in this matter and understand the line between Consanguinity and Affinity. Below is a helpful chart that shows you the different lines. Use this when calculating the legitimacy of a marriage or the lines of consanguinity and affinity.

102

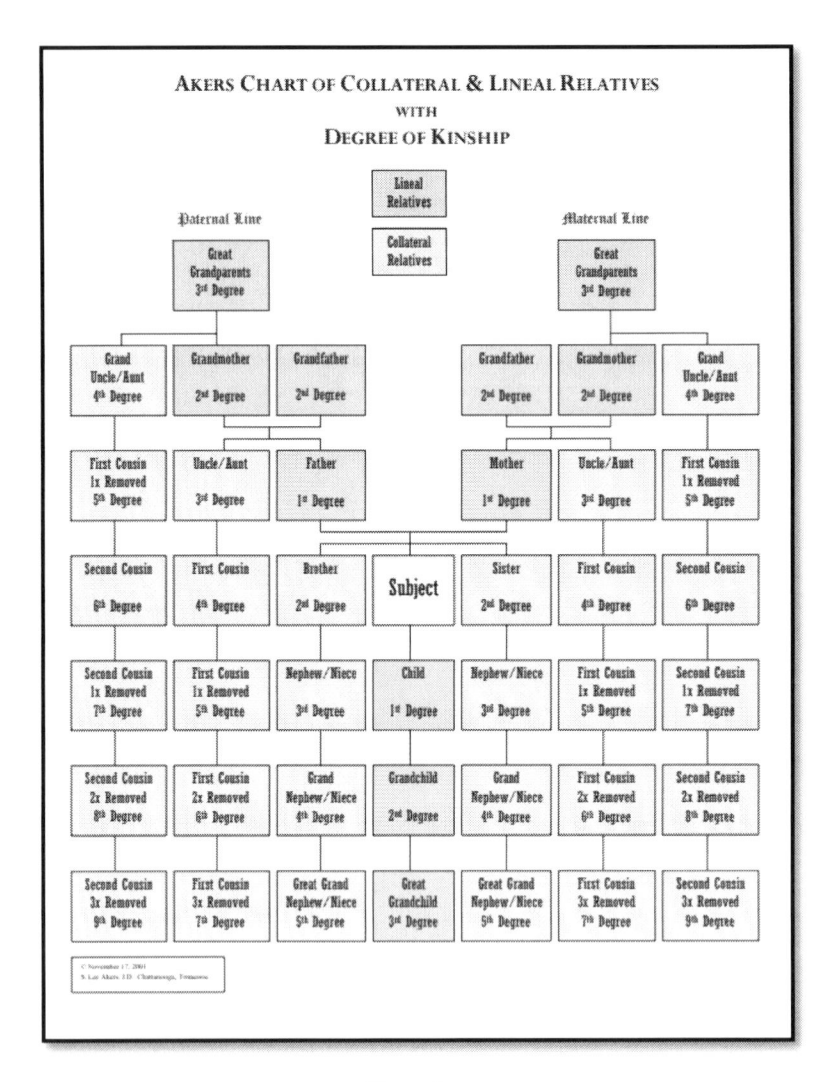

Figure 1

Akers Chart of Collateral & Lineal Relatives with Degree of Kinship

file:///C:/Users/bisho/OneDrive/Desktop/CHART%20-%20Akers%20Chart%20of%20Collateral%20and%20Lineal%20Relatives%20with%20Degree%20of%20Kinship.pdf

The Introduction of Customs as an Impediment

In Chapter 9 of Archbishop Scuderi's text: Interjurisdictional Canon Law-Volume 1: Introduction to Interjurisdictional Canon Law for the Independent and Ecumenical Catholic Churches, he details Customs under the Law. Customs are practices or lifestyles that are common among any community. Laws grow out of customs. Scuderi (2022, pg.181) states, *"The culture of the people is to be considered when creating a Code of Canon Law. If the law does not apply to the culture and the culture cannot apply itself to the law, the law is null and void and does not act as a protection for the people, but rather a babbling discourse that is meaningless nomenclature, and will not be adhered to nor followed....The interpretation of law should be done using culture."*

In themselves, customs do not dictate law and they do not create laws. They influence the development of laws. Community customs do not create, negate, or obliterate marriage laws. That is up to society. However, Church communities (denominations, etc.) must follow the regulations and laws concerning marriage as they are purported by sociological dictates and standards. In theory, customs may have the force of law, but only if that custom conforms to the law according to that civilly legislated community. To illustrate this, the impediment called, *disparity of cult* where two people of different religions get married and now want a divorce, came out of a cultural mandate, not a church mandate (CLSA, Canon Law a Text and Commentary, 1985, pg.759). Therefore, if a church faith tradition, which can be called a cultural custom, does not include a *disparity of cult* in their Code of Canon Law, then *disparity of cult* does not exist and should not be admissible into evidence if such a case comes about except if one of the parties, in their denomination's Code of Canon Law has the impediment of *disparity of cult*, then it should be brought into evidence during divorce proceedings.

In some churches, the Ordinary or Chief Administrator (whatever they call themselves) can be very powerful and dictate who can and cannot get married. Some local churches or an entire denomination, depending on how that church's Code of Canon Law reads, can prohibit marriages of their members for *serious (just) causes*. If this is the case, the onus is on the Ordinary or Chief Administrator to illustrate and define *just cause*. If the *just cause* does not go against society's marriage laws, those seeking the marriage need to decide if they wish to stay in that denomination or not, but they cannot be prohibited to marry if they choose. It may be invalid in the Church's eyes, but in the eyes of the State, the marriage is both valid and licit.

If, for example, the marriage of the couple may lead to scandal, the type of scandal needs to be determined. If the scandal is one that only embarrasses the church but is not considered a scandal under normal sociological standards, folkways, and mores, then, again, the couple will have to decide if they want to get married and leave that church or not get married and stay in the church. In Interjurisdictional Canon Law, the church has no right to dictate to anyone who wants to get married, if they can or cannot get married unless there is a clear and present danger to the couple, society, or both. Just because a church sees something as improper, does not mean a society sees things in the same vein. For the Interjurisdictional Lawyer, the consequences of the couple's actions concerning the church need to be clearly outlined and explained in accordance with the State, County, or Countries customs underlying marriage.

Only for serious cause should an Ordinary or Church interfere in a couple getting married. Suspicion is not, *just cause* for ecclesiastical interference. For an Ordinary to interfere into the acceptance or rejection of officiating at the marriage of a couple must be *beyond a reasonable doubt*. Proof *beyond a reasonable doubt* is the highest standard of proof and requires that only people who are truly guilty through the presentation of incontrovertible evidence, are truly guilty. If this is proven the person is found guilty in an American Court of Law, and in the case of Church law, the Ordinary, or Chief Administrator may show cause why the couple cannot marry. If this occurs, then it is within the Church's right to mandate that none of its clergy marry that couple.

Impediments to Marriage derived from Divine Law vs. Ecclesiastical Law (a brief clarification).

To summarize the above concerning divine and ecclesiastical law, *divine law* can be seen as natural law. If it goes against nature, it should not happen. For example, Mothers should not marry their sons, Fathers should not marry their daughters and brothers should not marry their sisters (see the chart above concerning the affinity lines). *Divine laws* that are violated, regardless of the denomination or their belief system are never, in Interjurisdictional Law, to be argued for a dispensation. If ecclesiological law agrees with Divine Law then ecclesiological laws may never be dispensed. If they do not agree with Divine Law and are a construct of the human hand, there is room for debate even if the denomination in their Canons says that ecclesiastical law may never be dispensed. Usually, however, ecclesiastical issues can be dispensed by high church officials or the legislative authority of that denomination. The exception to this is *diriment* impediments, discussed above which invalidates any attempt at a marriage or is prohibited by State and local Civil laws.

As a review, there are other distinctions in the realm of marital impediments.

1. ***Public Impediments*** are proven in the external forum, meaning society can prove that there are issues that may cause scandal or are inappropriate in natural (divine) law.

2. ***Occult Impediments*** An "occult impediment" to marriage is one that cannot be proven. It is not public. In Roman Canon Law (canon 1047), an occult impediment is unlike a public impediment that can be proven. The occult impediment may not be able to be proven. An example of this may be proof of a public impediment that may be viewed in authenticated public records and may be brought into evidence.

    An example of an occult impediment would be consanguinity resulting from a union that was illicit. Consanguinity means "blood relation", It is the property of being from the same kinship as another person. In that aspect, consanguinity is the quality of being descended from the same ancestor as another person (see, Figure 1 above).

3. *Holy Orders* in some denominations can be viewed as an impediment to marriage. This impediment may be resolved through a dispensation of Holy Orders, usually by the Presiding Bishop. In the case of a Roman Catholic Priest, it must be dispensed by the Apostolic See (Rome).

4. *Public Perpetual Vow of Chastity* that their church views as a permanent vow and not just simple vows are an impediment to marriage. In most independent denominations and churches outside the Roman Catholic Church, Buddhist church, and a few others, Public Perpetual Solemn Vows for a Layperson, such as those taken by the Third Order of Franciscan Friars (aka the Lay Franciscan) is not an impediment to marriage. They do not take a perpetual vow of Chastity though some may choose to take a "vow" of Chastity or "Promise" of Chastity. In those cases, the person is choosing to be celibate or chaste, which impedes marriage unless they are released from that vow or promise by the appropriate church authority.

5. *Abductions* of people who are forced against their will to marry are an impediment to marriage. In these cases, even if a "marriage ceremony" takes place and the person abducted

says "I do," that marriage is invalid and illicit because they are forced against their will.

6. *Crime,* usually the murder of a spouse, is an impediment to marriage. An example of this is two people who are married. One of the spouses falls in love with another person and, either by their own hand or another's through a contract, murders their spouse to marry another is an impediment.

> If a person decides to marry, someone under false pretenses is an impediment to marriage. An illustration of this is the married person in Philadelphia who goes on a business trip and marries another person in Kentucky but never tells that person they are married and never tells his spouse that he or she intends to marry someone in another state. This is both illegal by civil law and a canonical impediment.

> If either or both parties are in an adulterous relationship and decide to marry the person they are having an affair with, regardless of shared information to the other that a dual relationship is occurring, this is an impediment to a marriage and a crime in society. This also includes if, in the adulterous relationship, the adulterer has their "real" spouse killed off so they can marry.

> In Eastern Law, there is a crime that creates an invalidating impediment to marriage, "namely, those who, during the term of the same lawful marriage, commit adultery with each other and give each other a mutual promise of marriage or

actually attempt marriage, even though by a merely a civil act (MP. Can. 65 in Hueles, 1986, pg.191).

7. *Consanguinity* means that the parties to be married are too closely related by blood. There are two types of consanguinity, Ecclesiastical, and Divine and that depends on the degree of the relationship (see above Figure 1 for references).

"In the Direct Line marriage is invalid between all ancestors and descents both legitimate and natural" (Huels, 1986).

As noted above, direct line consanguinity are the blood relationships between direct ancestors and their descents. This is best seen in Akers chart (Figure 1) above. Collateral Consanguinity "is when two persons have a common ancestor, but neither is the direct ancestor of the other, e.g., brother and sister, uncle and niece, first cousins, second cousins, etc. (Huels, 1986). The Impediment occurs in the direct and collateral lines of consanguinity in the following relationships:

    a. Direct and Collateral lines

    b. Second Degree Consanguinity: brothers and sisters

    c. Third Degree Consanguinity: aunt, nephew, uncle, and niece

    d. Fourth Degree Consanguinity: great aunt, great uncle, and grandniece

Figure 2 below is the table of consanguinity. This chart should be helpful in determining the lines of impediments.

Table of Consanguinity
Showing degrees of relationship

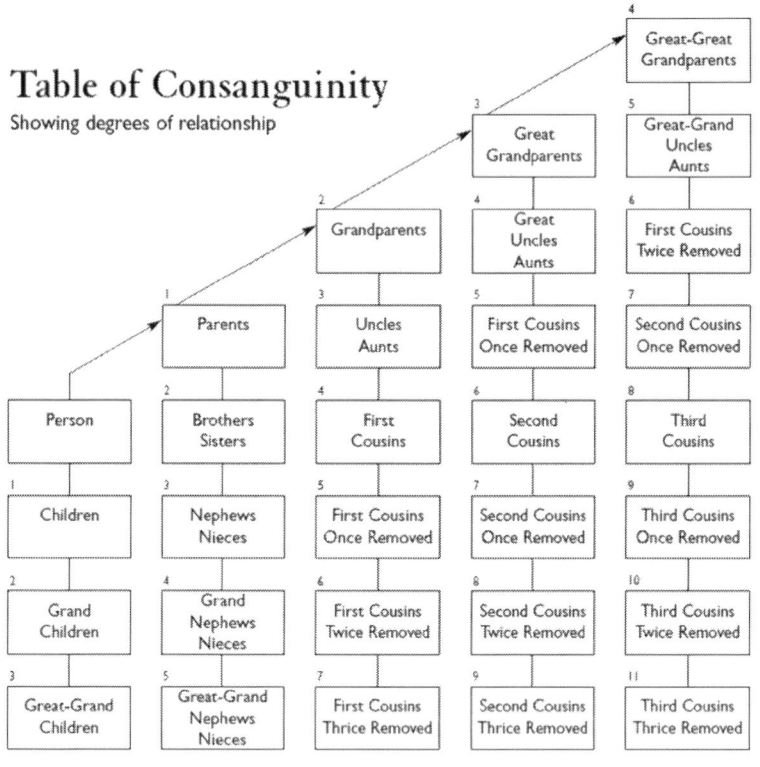

	Person	Brothers Sisters	Uncles Aunts	Great Uncles Aunts	Great-Grand Uncles Aunts	Great-Great Grandparents
		Parents	Grandparents	Great Grandparents		
1	Children	Nephews Nieces	First Cousins	First Cousins Once Removed	First Cousins Twice Removed	
2	Grand Children	Grand Nephews Nieces	First Cousins Once Removed	Second Cousins	Second Cousins Once Removed	
3	Great-Grand Children	Great-Grand Nephews Nieces	First Cousins Twice Removed	Second Cousins Once Removed	Third Cousins	
			First Cousins Thrice Removed	Second Cousins Twice Removed	Third Cousins Once Removed	
				Second Cousins Thrice Removed	Third Cousins Twice Removed	
					Third Cousins Thrice Removed	

Figure 2

Table of Consanguinity

(Jennifer Wilderson, Esq, J.D.

http://www.jwilkerson.net/the-czech-republic-and-consanguinity/)

"The general rule for calculating the degree is to count the number of persons taken together on both lines but without counting the common ancestor" (Hueles, 1986). Here is how it works:

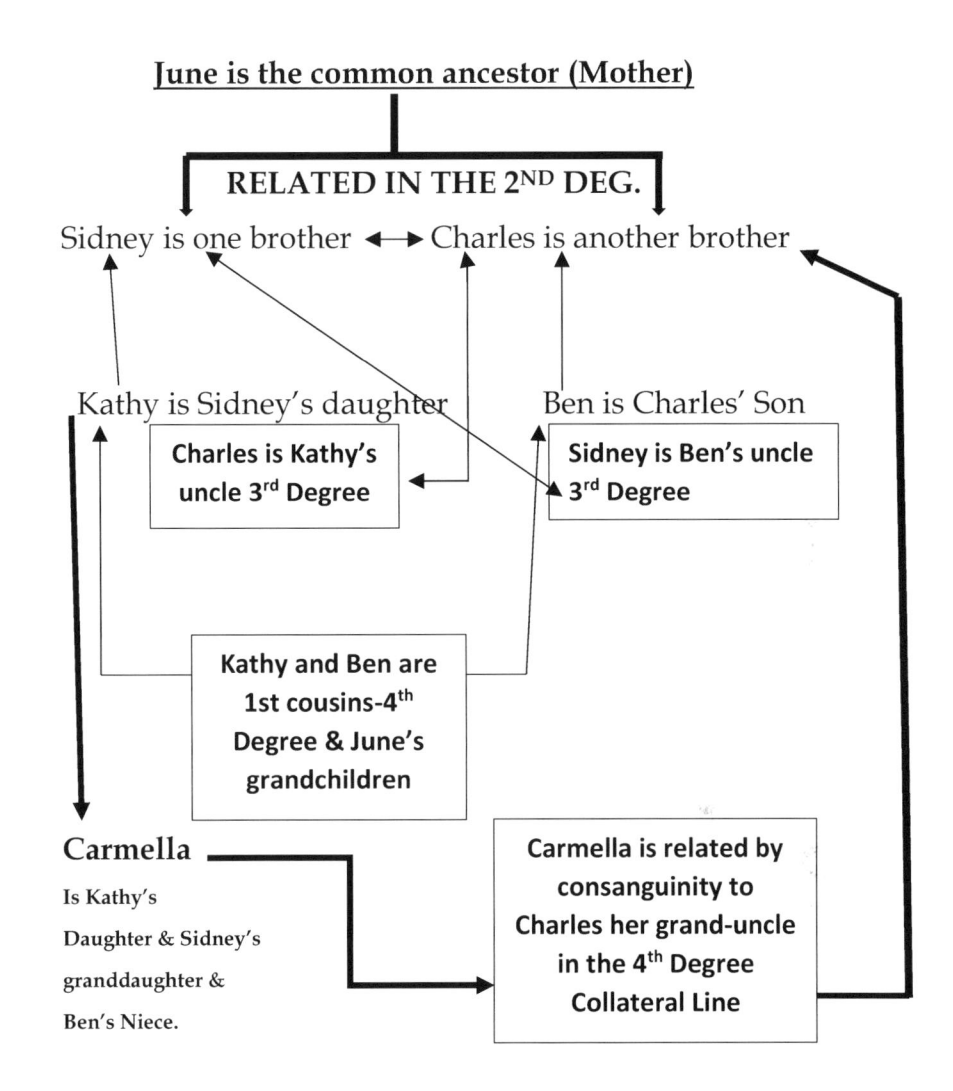

June is the common ancestor (Mother)

RELATED IN THE 2ND DEG.

Sidney is one brother ↔ Charles is another brother

Kathy is Sidney's daughter

Ben is Charles' Son

Charles is Kathy's uncle 3rd Degree

Sidney is Ben's uncle 3rd Degree

Kathy and Ben are 1st cousins-4th Degree & June's grandchildren

Carmella

Is Kathy's Daughter & Sidney's granddaughter & Ben's Niece.

Carmella is related by consanguinity to Charles her grand-uncle in the 4th Degree Collateral Line

---

How it works

1. June, the Mother, is the common ancestor to Sidney and Charles, her two sons making Sidney and Charles brothers in the second degree (not noted above).
2. Kathy is Sidney's daughter and Ben is Charles's son
3. Charles is Kathy's uncle (3rd degree) and Sidney is Ben's uncle (3rd degree)
4. Kathy and Ben are first cousins (4th degree) and the grandchildren of June
5. Carmella is Kathy's daughter and Sidney's granddaughter, Ben's niece.
6. Carmella is related by consanguinity to Charles her grand uncle in the 4th degree collateral line consanguinity.

8. **Affinity**

If a marriage is valid, even if not yet consummated, and exists between a man and a blood relative of his wife and simultaneously between a woman and the blood relations of her husband Affinity arises. This is known as an *in-law relationship* and exists *"only between the husband and the blood relative of the wife and between the wife and blood relative of the husband. Affinity is computed as follows: The blood relatives of the husband are related by affinity to the wife in the same line and degree as they are related by consanguinity to the husband and vice versa. To compute affinity, therefore, one need only determine the line and degree of consanguinity, because it is exactly the same line and degree for affinity. Thus, a man is related to his mother by consanguinity in t first degree of the direct line; his wife is related to his mother (her mother-in-law) by affinity also in the first degree of the direct line"* (Huels, 1986, pg.26).

How it works

1. June is the Mother
2. Sidney is the son (first line direct consanguinity)
3. Sidney is married to Ginella
4. June is the mother-in-law to Ginella
5. Ginella is related to June in the 1st Degree Direct Line Consanguinity because she is married to Sidney who, by virtue of being

June's son, is 1st Degree Direct Line Consanguinity.

Another example of how affinity works

1. Charles is Sidney's brother
2. Sidney is married to Ginella
3. Charles is related by *affinity* to Ginella in the 2nd Degree Collateral Consanguinity
4. Ramona is the 1st Cousin to Ginella
5. Ramona is related to Sidney, Ginella's husband, in the 4th degree Collateral Line Consanguinity

9. **Public Propriety**

Public propriety causes an impediment when a man and women are living together and the women is a known concubine, and vice versa (the man is a known male prostitute) and they are not married. If the man decides he wants to marry the woman's mother, or the woman decides she wants to marry the man's father or son, but not each other, even if the one of the cohabiting couples were to die, this causes what is known as a *public propriety impediment* and depending on the canons of the church the Interjurisdictional canon lawyer is dealing with, they cannot be married, and this marriage is deemed invalid. The key here is that either of the couples is a notorious individual guilty of concupiscence (a known prostitute).

To have a marriage deemed invalid it has to have at least the appearance of a marriage that is invalid for some reason or another. The issue of an impediment arises only if the couple begins to live together outside of wedlock.

According to Hueles (1986, pg. 195), *"Concubinage is had when two persons live as husband and wife for the purpose of habitually having sexual intercourse, the union however not having even the appearance of marriage. For the impediment to arise it is necessary that the concubinage be notorious or public., i.e., well known to the community."*

In Eastern Church law, the impediment of public Propriety extends to the second degree of the direct line consanguinity (Mp. Can. 69).

10. **Adoption**

If the parties are related by adoption they cannot be married. Eastern Canon Law, Roman Catholic Canon Law and most other Independent Churches agree with this because of the legal relationship between anyone in the adopted family and the adopted individual.

In Civil law, an invalidating impediment in Puerto Rico and Massachusetts prohibits adoptive marriages between the adopting parent and the adopted child (even if that child is of legal age at the time of adoption). Mississippi prohibits marriages between a father and his adoptive daughter (Doyle, CLSA, Commentary, pp. 774). If, however, people immigrate from another country they are subject to the laws of the country they come from. In other words, if a father marries his adopted daughter and the country of origin allows this and they decided to come to America, they may remain married. They follow the law of the country of origin.

11. Spiritual Relationship

A godparent may or may not be able to marry their godson or goddaughter depending on the denomination. Check the Canon Laws of the denomination. For example, the Eastern Catholic Churches apply this dictum, but the Roman Catholic Church does not. This impediment to marriage also exists in the Eastern Church where those disqualified for marriage by civil law because they are guardians cannot validly marry under Canon Law (See Mp. Cn. 71).

There are other factors that can invalidate a marriage that needs to be reviewed in each denomination's Codes of Canon Law. Some of these invalidating categories include *Lack of form*. This is when a marriage in most Catholic denominations, both Latin and Independent and possibly in some Eastern Churches, takes place without following the rubrics and laws that govern the celebration of marriage. If the ceremony does not come close to even resembling what a marriage ceremony should look like, that marriage is invalid but may be considered licit in the Civil realm.

As mentioned above, to review briefly, *coercion* is an impediment to marriage. Two people must be free to marry, of appropriate age and without undue pressure. The only way the impediment can be removed is if it is proven that both couples have agreed to the marriage freely. This includes freely without being convinced through psychological manners. An illustration of this is a cult leader that convinces a person to marry them because it is the right thing to do. This is called *undue influence*.

According to Investopedia, Undue influence occurs when an individual is able to persuade another's decisions due to the relationship between the two parties. Often, one of the parties is in a position of power over the other due to elevated status, higher education, or emotional ties. The more powerful individual uses this advantage to coerce the other individual into making decisions that might not be in their long-term best interest.

Undue influence is an equitable doctrine that involves one person taking advantage of a position of power over another person. This inequity in power between the parties can vitiate one party's consent as they are unable to freely exercise their independent will. In exerting undue influence, the influencing individual is often able to take advantage of the weaker party. In contract law, a party claiming to be the victim of undue influence may be able to void the terms of the agreement (Hayes, 2022 in Investopedia).

Psychological immaturity or mental incapacity is an impediment to marriage. The couple being married must be of sound mind and body to be validly and licitly married. They must understand what they are doing as it applies both sacramentally and civilly. They must have the capacity to accept all responsibilities that accompany the vows of marriage.

Refusal to have children is a choice. Both couples may choose not to have children, but still, wish to be married. For some denominations, this may present an impediment and invalidate the marriage. However, in society today and in most interdenominational and independent churches this is not an issue. Now, if the situation arises where one of the couples wants children and the other person refuses to have intercourse and deprives the other of children that may, depending on the denomination constitute an impediment to marriage and invalidate the nuptial union. However, in other denominations, the whole idea of marriage is for the procreation of the next generation, and the refusal to have children is viewed as not for the good of the marriage or relationship. If the couple is capable of fathering and mothering children and to their understanding, the woman is capable of becoming pregnant and carrying the child to birth and chooses not to have children that may or may be an impediment. However, if the mother is capable of conception and the man refuses to have intercourse that may constitute an impediment according to that denomination's Code of Canon Law. In the Roman Catholic Church, One of the goods of marriage is children. A man or woman physically capable of fathering or, respectively, conceiving a child but who intends never to have children may not marry in the Catholic Church.

Marital impediments and prohibitions to marriage are found in the Book of Leviticus and diverse ancient canonical texts that distinguish between diriment impediments rendering a marriage null and void, and prohibitory impediment rendering marriages merely valid but illicit (Boucinhan, 1910). Not until the twelfth century do we see the term *impediment* used. Gratian in his Decretals (see Scuderi, Volume 1-Preface, 2022) nor Peter Lombard in his Sentences (Amazon- KDP Series, 2010). By 1190 Bernard freely uses the term *impediment* in the classic phrase, *impedit contrahendum et dirimit contractus (prevents the contract and invalidates the contract)*. Bernard continues to enumerate the impediments as he writes: *sunt autern quae matrimoniun impediunt (while there are those who impede marriage)* (Boucinhan, 1910).

As the continuum of time advanced, the distinction between diriment and prohibitory impediments of marriage encountered a sharp division with fairly successful attempts to clarify and classify diriment impediments.

As a review here is a list of impediments of marriage in an arrangement that seems to be the most logical and complete:

1. Prohibitory Impediments: Render a marriage illicit but valid.

2. Betrothal: Validly engages the couple. At one point this bound the man to marry that woman and no other unless the betrothal was broken in some manner.

3. Vow: A vow of chastity, simple or solemn, constituted a diriment impediment because

a vow is seen as between the person and God and an obstacle to any marriage.

4. Mixed Marriages: A marriage between a baptized and non-baptized person, or a Roman Catholic and baptized non-Roman Catholic. This is the object of a prohibitory impediment (mixo religio: mixed religion) and is viewed as a relative impediment.

5. Vetitum Ecclesiae: This is an ecclesiastical prohibition imposed on the person by a precept affecting only the capacity of an individual due to some type of character defect. It is imposed to delay marriage until conditions have been fulfilled by the individual. Once fulfilled the marriage can take place (This goes back to the concept of Betrothal above. Once the betrothal has been dissolved, then the person can marry)

6. Forbidden Times *(tempus clausum, tempus feriatum [time close, holiday time])*: This impediment does not affect the personal capacity of the couple contracted in marriage. It prohibits the solemn celebration of the marriage therefore, forbidding the marriage to take place (this is an impediment not in place today but was common during the council of Trent, 1545-1563 Session XXIV, cap.x "De Reform. Matrim.")

7. Diriment impediments: Rendering a marriage null and void and there were three types:

      a. Type 1: Personal incapacities rising from the physicality of the person: *impuberty and impotency* (Puberty is viewed as age 12 for girls and 14 for boys)

      b. Type 2: Only diriment impediments based only on form, to wit, and clandestinely.

      c. Type 3: Impediments (improperly called impediments) caused by a defect of consent arising from mental incapacity (ignorance-*confuso* [confused] and insanity); or Error (*error personae*), making a mistake relating to the person's liberty (*conditio servilis*) or a quality that effected a person (*redundans in personam*), or marriage by an unjust force causing a forced (not free) consent (*vis et metus*) and finally if a consent real or not, is destroyed by adding to the contract clauses conditions contrary to the essential elements of marriage such as divorce, adultery (aka: an open relationship). However, a mere concomitant intention is not a cause for nullity.

The last issue to be considered in marriage law is that of fidelity of each spouse. If either of the parties decides not to be faithful in the relationship before the wedding, yet go through with the wedding ceremony, they are not validly married and that marriage in Interdenominational Canon Law is an illicit marriage. However, the civil authorities may deem the marriage a valid union with exceptions if it is discovered that deceit was part of the mindset of one or the other who were married.

Nullity

It should be understood that Marriage is a lifelong commitment between two people. It is a legal and binding contract. The normal marriage has its ups and downs. There are good times and bad times. Feelings get hurt, anger abates, and frustrations happen. However, through all this there are wonderful times. For some it is the beginning of a new life. A family is formed Children are created and life moves forward.

Unfortunately, there are those times when, for numerous reasons, marriages just don't work. When two people come to an impasse in their lives, grow apart, or never should have been married in the first place, there are remedies. In Civil society, the marriage contract can be broken through the process called divorce. It is a lengthy process and could be rather expensive. Most churches have an issue with divorce. They believe that no matter what, once the commitment is made, nothing should break it asunder. Some churches will even excommunicate the person or couple because of the divorce. Others may deprive the person or couple from receiving any of the sacraments except the Sacrament of Reconciliation.

In some cases, two people may enter into a marriage when they should not. It is just a bad match and to stay in that marriage would be detrimental to the couple, society, and the church. In these instances, the church provides the annulment process (and so do most States in the United States). For an annulment to happen, the couple must meet certain conditions because the church believes that it cannot separate what has been united by God (EWTN, 2018). The church, however, also believes that with God's help and the guidance of Canon Law, a marriage can be dissolved if it meets certain criteria. In some churches, the canons may not address this issue or outright not say anything about a divorce. It just doesn't matter. The Gospel of Matthew 19:5-6 and Paul's letter to the Corinthians in 1 Cor 7:10-11 lay out certain conditions that provide for a canonically valid marriage contract. If one of the parties were prohibited from marrying, possibly they are already married but never tell the other person, or for some other reason, there is a *diriment impediment*. This invalidates the marriage in the eyes of the church and the union is annulled. Because diriment impediments are not known the marriage is called a *putative marriage* if at least one of the parties married in good faith.

A marriage is valid unless proven otherwise (CLSA, 1983, cn. 1083). Marriages can be invalid from the start. Other than a diriment impediment (see above), there are four things that can make a marriage defective from the start. These four areas are, *Defect of Form, Defect of Contract, Defect of Will,* and *Defect of Capacity.*

The first consideration for nullification is *Defect of Form.*

Chapter 4

The Sacrament of Holy Orders

The Effect of the Sacrament of Holy Orders

The Sacrament of Holy Orders is performed sacramentally through liturgy and takes effect through the words of ordination or consecration and the laying on of hands.

Each sacrament has its own definitions and criteria that have been discussed previously in this or in another Volume of Interjurisdictional Canon Law. Therefore, we will not go into detailed definitions of the sacrament. The only Holy Order we will define a bit is that of Deacon since there are two types of diaconal states, *Transitional and Permanent.* Other than the diaconate, all other Holy Orders are to be done only by a Bishop or, when consecrating someone to the Episcopacy, be aware of the denomination's Code of Canon Law. For example, the Apostolic Episcopal Church's canons state that only One bishop is needed to consecrate another bishop, but three bishops are the preference. Some Orthodox churches require a minimum of two to consecrate and traditionally there are three bishops. The tradition of three bishops evolved from the question what if the main consecrator is invalid? Then the consecration would not be valid, but if you have two or three bishops and during the ceremony, all three lay hands, then the power of the episcopacy is transferred and even though the main celebrant wasn't valid or licit, one of the other probably are.

General Definitions of Holy Orders

Holy Orders can be achieved through the traditional diocesan seminary training, or the preparation and seminary based formation of candidates for holy orders of a religious community which has the added as part of the formative years a pre-novitiate, novitiate, Solemn Profession, followed by Theological Studies then onto Holy Orders. Some churches do not have a sequence of "minor orders" but move from seminary training straight to ordination. There may be some Catholic denominations that may not even require seminary training but some form of mentoring. It is best, if an issue arises concerning the legitimacy of Holy Orders or some form of irregularity or impediment, always confer to the denominations Code of Canon Law. For those who have a sequence of "minor orders" before the conferral of "major orders", both "minor" and "major" orders are introduced below.

There is a sequence to the reception of Holy Orders. The first set is usually done throughout seminary training are *Porter, Reader,* and *Acolyte*. These are called *minor orders*. Normally, they are given to the ordination candidates throughout their Theological studies, one after the completion of each year of study. There are exceptions where all of the minor orders are given at one time. Though rare, this does happen and is completely valid and licit. For those to whom these *minor orders* apply, they are usually conferred by what we will call an *Administrative Appointee*. This individual can be a formation director, superior, or someone appointed by the diocesan bishop to confer the orders. A bishop is not needed to confer the minor orders. It is rare, but not impossible, that any impediments or irregularities occur at this stage. They are straightforward, and the process of conferral starts with observing the candidate and appropriately scrutinizing their worthiness according to the rubrics and Canon Laws of the particular denomination. At one point and instill in some denominations there is the additional *minor order* of Exorcist. Traditionally, the order of Exorcist is granted and then removed by the bishop. If someone is qualified later in their vocation to be an Exorcist, the order is reinstated and granted by a bishop. Technically, a bishop should never be an Exorcist. This can be very dangerous for the bishop on many levels not to be discussed here. If interested, please refer to literature about becoming and functioning as an Exorcist in whatever denomination interests the reader. That said, once the minor orders are complete, and the seminarian becomes eligible for the entrance into Holy Orders, the first step in *major order* is the *Deaconate*.

The Permanent Diaconate

Only a Bishop may ordain a Deacon. There are two types of Deacons. The first is the *Permanent Deacon*. The Deacon, before being ordained must complete adequate seminary training and formation. It is the duty of the Diocesan Bishop or Formation Directors to ensure that adequate and appropriate training has occurred. The vocation to the *Permanent Deaconate* implies that this individual does not wish to become a *Presbyter (Priest)*. Once they are ordained a

Permanent Deacon, they are a Deacon for life. In the Roman Catholic Tradition, and some other Catholic traditions the *Lay Permanent Deacon* may be married and have a family. They function and have the same powers granted them as a traditional celibate *Transitional Deacon.* Please be careful if issues arise with transitional deacons. Carefully read the denomination's Canon Laws governing the Office of Permanent Deacon, especially where the Lay Permanent Deacon is a parishioner who wishes to do service to the church as a deacon and is married. A problem may arise if the canons of the church you are working with states where a lay deacon may be married, but if their spouse dies, they cannot remarry. Canon 33 of the Roman Code of Canon Law (1983), for Example states clearly, " It is decided that marriage be altogether be prohibited to bishops, priests, and deacons, or to all clerics placed in the ministry, and that they keep away from their wives and not beget children' whoever does this shall be deprived of the honor of the clerical office." Transitional deacons may not marry before or after they are ordained and cannot according to Rome be ordained until after their 25th birthday. If the spouse of a deacon does die and the canons read that deacon must not remarry and remarries, the church usually rescinds the Order of Deacon, and that person may not function as a Deacon. However, there are other churches that do not have this canon. If a spouse dies remarriage is allowed without penalty. If orders are rescinded, and that person attempts to engage the services of an Interjurisdictional Canon Lawyer, the only thing the lawyer can do is to advise the person of the law and render support. There is no case in this instance unless there is a Canon that states the contrary and the deacon is released with prejudice. At that point, the services of the Interjurisdictional Canon Lawyer may be employed to argue the case for reinstatement for the defendant.

In some denominations within the independent church movement, this is not an issue. At any level, a clergyperson may marry. The cleric has the option of being a permanent or transitional deacon. The criteria usually remain the same, that is, if the cleric chooses to be a permanent deacon they are a permanent deacon for life, and if that person chooses to go onto the presbyterate, they may enjoy the transitional diaconate.

The Transitional Diaconate

A *transitional deacon* is a deacon that has completed their seminary studies according to their church law or religious formation in accordance with their church laws that govern the ordination to the priesthood and is preparing for *Presbyteral Orders* (The Priesthood). Like the *Permanent Deacon*, only a Bishop may ordain this individual through the anointing and the laying on of hands. There is no such thing as *ordination by proxy*. This person has completed all their studies and is usually assigned to a ministry in their last year's summer to get a sense of what ministry comprises. Upon election to the *transitional diaconate*, following their canonical time as a deacon, the *transitional deacon* has been duly prepared for the next major order, the *Presbyterate (Priesthood)*.

Again, it is of utmost importance that the Interjurisdictional Canon Lawyer review and understand the canons of the denomination that govern the state of the *transitional deacon* as married clergy or not. For denominations such as The Ecumenical Catholic Church of Christ, it does not matter if the deacon is transitional or permanent they may be married and if their spouse dies, they are free to remarry and remain in the status of deacon ready to transition to the priesthood. Please check the canons of the church you will be dealing with if the remarriage criteria apply or if the spouse of a deacon dies, that deacon may remarry without prejudice.

The Deacon has liturgical and ministerial jobs. The Deacon visits the sick, Assists the Priest at Mass, and performs other liturgies like prayer services, communion services, distributes Holy Communion, preaches, reads the Gospel, and can do Baptisms and Marriages. However, the deacon cannot celebrate Mass or hear confessions or confirm even in extraordinary circumstances.

The Form of the Sacrament

Every faith tradition Catholic or not has a liturgy (ceremony) for ordaining a Deacon. The words (the Form) of the ceremony, are prescribed in the denominations *Sacramentary* or *Missal* or other text that has liturgies. The book used by the Bishop to ordain the Deacon is called the *Pontifical* and has the *rubrics* (directions) for not only what and how things are said but also the directions on what to do when to do things, and how to do them. It is always a good thing to have a Master of Ceremonies handy when doing any form of the ministerial ceremony, so things are not inadvertently left out. In some cases, mistakes happen during the liturgy but that does not invalidate the liturgy. To illustrate this, this writer was involved as co-consecrator of a new bishopelect. During the consecration ceremony, the Book of the Gospels is supposed to be held over the head of the candidate. There was no Master of Ceremonies and instead of holding the book over his head, which we forgot to do, by accident, the main consecrator had the bishop-elect hold the Book of the Gospels (during rehearsal we practiced both, holding the book over his head and having him hold another Book of the Gospels). This little glitch did not invalidate the Consecration. To this day this wonderful bishop is enjoying his episcopacy serving the Persian Community throughout the world.

The Matter of the Sacrament

The laying on of hands and anointing with Holy Chrism by the Bishop as an invocation and infusion of the Holy Spirit is the Matter of the Sacrament.

Impediments, and Irregularities relevant to the Sacrament of Holy Orders to the Deaconate.

Part 1: Impediments

The word *impediment* is derived from the Latin word, *impedimentum* signifying whenever an embarrassment or hindrance occurs to a person. Whatever the issue may be that impedes the forward movement of the individual or the sacrament is an *impedimentum* or an *impediment*. In battle, the obstacle, be it slow or heavy artillery or, an overloaded backpack or duffle bag that caused the hindrance was called an *impedimenta*. In Canon Law, according to Boudinhon (1910), this term is applied *"to whatever hinders the free action of an agent, or to whatever prevents him from performing or at least form performing regularly, any act that the law takes cognizance of. The impediment therefore directly affects the juridical capacity of the agent, restrains it, or even entirely suppresses it; indirectly it affects the action itself, which it renders more or less defective or even null. An impediment consequently produces its effect by reason of defect; it ceases when the agent has legally recovered his capacity, whether that be by a dispensation or by his fulfilling the conditions requisite for the act he wishes to perform."*

Coming out of natural, human, civil, ecclesiastical, or Divine law, the impediment restricts or suppresses the juridical capacity of the person. When considering some issues such as nullifying a sacrament or action or reviewing a noticeable defect in a sacramental or other element performed during a liturgy, for example, *"in the case of a contract imposed by force on one of the parties, there would be no impediment unless in a wide improper sense of the term. This general idea of impediments is applicable to all those acts in regard to which the law regulates the juridical capacity of the agents; for instance, acquisition of jurisdiction, contracts in religious matters, and the sacraments(Boudinhon, 1910)."* Canonical examples of this include a layperson, heretic, or excommunicated person who is unable to acquire any type of spiritual jurisdiction. This may also include not yet emancipated children, religious under vows, and other carefully governed and supervised individuals and actions such as contractual agreements without permission from a superior or signing adult documents if not yet emancipated. Impediments also occur if rubrics are not followed in the sacraments and validity and liceity come into question, especially in the sacraments of matrimony and Holy Orders.

Technically there are restrictions on the use of the terms *impediment* and *irregularity*. In most instances, the term *impediment* refers to obstacles in a marriage and *irregularity* refers to obstacles to an Ordination. Boudinhon (1910) writes, *"thus, women and unbaptized persons, who are by Divine law incapable of being ordained, are not termed irregular. But speaking of matrimony, the word impediment refers to all obstacles, whether arising from natural or Divine law."*

Impediments to the priesthood are permanent unless removed by the highest church authority, and only the highest church authority (the Pope, Presiding Bishop, Primate, etc.). Priestly impediments are divided into *irregularities*. Simple *impediments* may pass with time without any action of the hierarchy. There are also impediments that may exist even after ordination. Some *irregularities* may be removed by the Ordinary if they are simple and not major in nature with the exception of apostasy, heresy, schism, abortion, murder, secret, and existent marriages of clergy where the Code of Canon Law of the denomination insists on a celibate clergy.

Faith Traditions that Demand a Celibate Clergy

Some traditions may demand celibacy in order to enjoy Holy Orders. Most Independent churches do not. In most Independent churches anyone with any office may be married. This includes the Presiding Bishop.

In some instances, the codification of celibacy is done publicly according to the rubrics of the ordination ceremony. During the ceremony, the candidate usually professes individually to the bishop either the promise of celibacy (Basically, this chastity for a non-religious clergyperson made to the bishop) or, the vow of chastity (Basically, this is celibacy made directly to God usually made in religious communities at solemn vows or both solemn vows/professions, and ordinations).

Irregularities to Holy Orders

By definition, an *Irregularity "is a canonical impediment directly impeding the reception of tonsure, and holy orders, or preventing the exercise of orders already received"* (Catholic Encyclopedia, Retrieved 2006).

Impediments are a perpetual condition and are termed *irregularities* where Holy Orders are concerned. They may be derived from past sins or delicts making a person ineligible for Holy Orders even if they have undergone the Sacrament of Reconciliation and have been forgiven the sin, but forgiveness of sin does not negate some church's dispensation from the irregularity. In some conservative churches, an irregularity may have occurred before baptism or, not with that denomination, after being received into that denomination, the irregularity still exists. The Interjurisdictional Canon Lawyer will see this issue a great deal if one of the clients happens to be a Roman Priest or was a Roman Catholic Priest.

In general, if someone seeking Holy Orders has an impediment that can be removed, it is done by order of the Presiding Bishop or highest authority within that denomination. If a dispensation is granted, this intimates that the church accepts that whatever impeded that person from entering Holy Orders is no longer an issue and that person may enter Holy Orders validly and licitly. The requirement for lifting a dispensation depends on the violation that got them the irregularity in the first place. Depending on the type of impediment or irregularity and the denomination's canon laws, some may be removed easily by the Ordinary of the Diocese whereas others may be removed only by the Presiding Bishop or highest church official.

Remember, with any irregularity or impediment, even with remorse, a church does not have the obligation to dispense anyone. They have the privilege to dispense. A person who may come to the Interjurisdictional Canon Lawyer looking for a case against a church on the grounds of prejudice from the refusal of the church to remove an impediment or irregularity has no case unless it can be proven beyond a reasonable doubt that the impediment or irregularity was imposed by the church onto the person for reasons other than canonical violations.

Below are examples based on Roman Catholic Canon Law of impediments and remission of the impediment. This will give the reader an idea of what an impediment or irregularity is, and, how it can be dispensed. Churches may have other items in their Codes of Canon Law that resemble these but call them something different. Regardless, the key is to remember that these violations are very serious, can render someone impotent to receive any form of Holy Order and may be considered a permanent condition. Always refer to the denomination's Code of Canon Law for guidance where any form of impediment or irregularity is involved.

The Irregularity Affiliated with Mental Illness

A clinical diagnosis of any form of mental illness that impairs a person from performing their duties as a cleric is an impediment. Be careful here. The Diagnostic and Statistical Manual of Mental Disorders (DSM), a document constantly in review and rewrite is the most current instrument put out by the American Psychiatric Association (APA) that defines diverse mental challenges that may cause serious impairments in a person's judgments. However, be very cautious when looking into this issue especially if you, the reader, are not a clinician who has worked with the mentally ill. For our intents and purposes licensure is not necessarily needed because lawyers do not diagnose. However, the lawyer must know where to go to have one of questionable character properly diagnosed, that being a psychiatrist or psychologist who are the most trained in diagnostics. If someone is either applying for entrance into a seminary, order or other state that will end up with Holy Orders, it is imperative that that person understand the gravity of their office and have a sound mind. If there is a question after Holy Orders, concerning this issue, and a cleric is censured, suspended, or close to excommunication, it is recommended that a full battery of psychological evaluations, done ONLY by a licensed psychologist be performed before a decision is made. Certain mental illness does not disqualify a person from the clerical state. One such illness, depending on the severity is depression. If it is treatable there is no reason why someone cannot function as a cleric. However, if the cleric's state of mind is in question, and the Interjurisdictional Canon Lawyer is called upon to defend or prosecute, get a full battery of psychological evaluations.

The mental status of a clergyperson is of tremendous concern. In modern times numerous clergy in all denominations have been charged with pedophilia and other sexually related crimes. Churches have been sued, and parishioners have left the church. The guilty have been imprisoned, and the victims have been traumatized to the point where they have their own mental health issues later in life. With proper comprehensive mental status examinations that are done by trained psychologists, a lot of issues in this area could have been prevented through an appropriate weeding out process. If not resolved, at least uncovered early enough to protect those who have been taken advantage. If a clergyperson is found to possess less than a stellar character in this area, it behooves the Interjurisdictional Canon Lawyer to report this person to the proper civil authorities for due process under the law, and to recommend to the denomination that they adopt a comprehensive mental health evaluation process that will uncover these issues early, in the hopes that such predatory behaviors be stopped at the outset.

Another *irregularity* concerns the individual who rejects or has been known to reject the faith and is publicly known or recognized as a notorious unbeliever who may not be admitted into Holy Orders. If the person recants and repents it is left up to the Diocesan Bishop or higher authority in the church up to and including the Presiding Bishop to decide if this individual is ready to proceed in studies towards Holy Orders. In the event that someone is already ordained and becomes an *apostate,* deemed a *heretic,* or is *schismatic* the church has the right to excommunicate this individual and in most cases makes that person ineligible for the priesthood or to be taken back into the same church ever.

In some churches, namely the Roman Catholic Church, if a person is married or gets married or attempts to marry despite an existing valid marriage or promise of celibacy or vow of chastity forms an irregularity. In the Roman church, this holds true even if the spouse dies. In the Orthodox Church, a person may not be a priest unless he is married, and his wife must be Orthodox since she plays a major role in the ministry. If the wife dies the priest should remarry to continue his ministry. If he does not remarry the church decides what to do with that priest. In some instances, the church may decide to remove him from the priesthood altogether.

If a person commits voluntary homicide or procured an effective abortion or was found to be complicit in the murder or abortion—any prior act, statement, financial support that contributed to an abortion or murder that was successful has committed an act that is considered an irregularity to Holy Orders. This can even include taking the woman to the abortion clinic and/or paying for the abortion. If, however, a person is paying State taxes, and some of those taxes are going to fund abortion clinics, that is not considered an impediment to Holy Orders since that person is not directly paying to fund the clinic, and failure to pay taxes will result in criminal proceedings on the civil level. Furthermore, it is not considered a positive contribution to the abortion.

A person who attempts suicide or self-mutilates, or by their own free will or is complicit in the mutilation of another has an irregularity to Holy Orders and may not be entered into Holy Orders. In some cases, suicide or mutilations are premeditated, as are some murders. Any attempt at suicide regardless of mental status may be viewed in some churches as an irregularity that disqualifies someone from attempting Holy Orders.

There is a distinguishing element that must be considered. There are different degrees of self-mutilation. Cases, where superficial cutting occurs, need to be reviewed carefully and evaluated considering the reason and mental status. This may not be an invalidating factor to consider one for Holy Orders and may not be considered an irregularity. The second form of self-mutilation is called, *graviter et dolose* (seriously and deceitfully) and is considered an *impediment*. This form of self-mutilation consists of things like the complete evisceration of a limb, self-castration, etc.

With the exception of practicing "doing a mass," "hearing a confession" or performing another "priestly function" in a seminary classroom as a means of learning, is considered an irregularity and that person may not be Ordained.

If a person poses as a priest, regardless of seminary training or not, and is not ordained and attempts to perform any liturgical act prior to being ordained a priest or consecrated a Bishop commits an irregularity and may not be considered for Ordination.

The Irregularities After Ordination to the Priesthood

A person can be accused of an irregularity if they accept and receive Holy Orders with an irregularity and that person does not reveal the irregularity, or it is discovered after the ordination that that person had an irregularity. If the irregularity is not brought to the attention of the Bishop before the ordination so the Bishop can decide to dispense the irregularity and allow the ordination or stay the irregularity and forbid the ordination, that priest is validly and licitly ordained, providing the Bishop has proper intent to ordain, but that priest may not function as a priest. That is, he or she may not exercise their ministry until that irregularity has been removed.

After a person is ordained, if the person becomes an *apostate, heritic, or schizmatic* and it is publicly known (a notorious crime), that imposes an irregularity and is forbidden to perform any liturgical act or action. In some cases, that person is excommunicated. Depending on the church and the Bishop this may be a permanent removal.

Finally, if a person knowingly and willingly commits an action that either constitutes or leads to an irregularity, that person may not perform any liturgical acts or actions. Again, depending on the church and the Bishop, this irregularity may be removed.

Simple Impediments Blocking Ordination

For some Latin Rite churches affiliated with Rome, in particular, priests, Bishops and Eastern Catholic Bishops only who have been previously married must have the marriages nullified and voided, or the spouse has died. If the spouse has died, Bishops usually require that the children be raised to adulthood and on their own before the person can undertake studies for the priesthood.

In some churches, the Code of Canon Law forbids any Ordained Minister to hold public office. Review the codes before deciding to hear a case or prosecute a case. There may be nuances that allow the clergyperson to hold a political office, but it may be unclear in the law and needs interpretation and clarification. At other times, political positions, or other positions that a priest is not permitted by law to occupy constitute a simple impediment to ordination and it can be removed when that person leaves or resigns office. However, if that person does leave or resign office and gets ordained, and then runs again for office and wins, that person may get censured due to this irregularity and is deemed incapable of dispensing any sacrament or acting in any capacity as a priest.

Periodically, a neophyte recently baptized may feel the calling to the priesthood. This is a good thing. However, that person may not be mature enough or ready to take upon him or herself the responsibilities of the priesthood. In such cases of a simple irregularity, the Bishop will decide when that person is mature enough and ready to proceed onto Holy Orders.

In the event that a person has any *simple impediment* and receives Holy Orders, that impediment must be removed by a Bishop or that person cannot dispense any sacraments or act in the capacity of a priest until that impediment is removed.

If the ordained person contracts a mental disorder that hinders him or her to function as a priest or in society hindering him or her from the performance of their duties, that person may not dispense the sacraments or act in the capacity as a priest until the Bishop determines that the priest is well enough to exercise his or her ministry.

Chapter 5

Dispensation Procedures

Many denominations have their own Code of Canon Law and procedures in place that discipline their clergy. In the event that issues, or confusion arises within the discipline this section of the text may be used as a starting point to alleviate issues surrounding dispensations, or forgiveness of a violation from the ecclesiastical superior. When confronted with how to litigate issues where there is one conflict between what is written in this text and what the canons of the denomination that the Interjurisdictional Canon Lawyer is dealing, always consult with the chief administrator of the denomination. Use what is presented below as a guideline to assist you in determining the proper way to proceed.

Dispensations are granted to individuals who have some form of irregularity (impediment) against them. Remember, some denominations may not call these offenses *irregularities* or even *impediments*. These terms are usually found in Latin Law (The Code of Canon Law, 1983 of the Roman Catholic Church or in some Orthodox Canon Laws). The Old Catholic Church, depending on the governing foundation (The Church of Utrecht or another) may or may not use these terms. Regardless of the term, to get through the confusion we will refer to violations as *irregularities* or *impediments* depending on the circumstance as described above.

Procedures to Dispense an Irregularity (Impediment)

As previously defined An *irregularity* is a canonical impediment directly impeding the reception of tonsure and holy orders or preventing the exercise of orders already received, and an *impediment* is a legal obstacle that prevents a sacrament from being performed either validly or licitly or both. In dealing with the priesthood the term *irregularity* is used and it encompasses the term *impediment*. An *irregularity* is an *impediment*.

If a priest has an *irregularity* that cleric may directly approach their superior (the diocesan bishop, religious superior, or presiding bishop, etc.) who has the faculties to release that person of their irregularity (known as a *dispensation*). Dispensations can be granted in two forms, *internally* and *externally*.

Dispensing in the External Forum

In some cases, all the cleric needs to do is contact the local Ordinary and discuss the *irregularity* with the Bishop or Archbishop. There may be some issues that the Diocesan Bishop cannot dispense, and those issues would most likely be presented to the Presiding Bishop. To determine where to go, consult the denomination's canon law and look at the type of *irregularity*. Within the description of the *irregularity*, there should be directions, procedures, and processes concerning where to go, and to whom to go to dispense.

The first thing to do when seeking a dispensation is to formally write to the ordinary explaining everything. Detail in the letter what happened to incur the *irregularity* and the role the cleric played in causing the *irregularity*. When designing your defense discuss the reasons believed to have the *irregularity* removed. Be very clear in the details. Once the letter is received, expect an investigation to be done by the Ordinary or the Ordinary's delegate. In the External Forum, this will take time. The Ordinary will direct the Canon Lawyer or delegate exactly what to do and give to that lawyer the evidence the Ordinary has that caused the delict or *impediment*. If grounds are discovered implementing the cleric or seminarian seeking Holy Orders, the Ordinary can order the seminarian to be dismissed and not allowed into Holy Orders. If this is the case, this cannot be appealed, and the Ordinary's decision is final. In the case of an Ordained Priest (or higher office), the process is usually the same. An investigation will be done, and the evidence will be brought forward. If culpability is discovered, the Ordinary can censure the cleric and that will stand. If a Bishop is charged, this matter must go to the Presiding Bishop for disposition. If the Presiding Bishop decides to hold the censure or other disposition that cannot be challenged. The only one who can reverse that decision is the Presiding Bishop. These issues do not go to the Ecclesiastical court.

In some instances, during the investigative process, in the evidentiary phase when evidence is being gathered, the Ordinary may refuse to grant Holy Orders to the candidate even if he or she has completed the prerequisite studies since ordination is a privilege and not a right. If there are questions during the discovery phase that may shed light on the non-culpability of the cleric, the cleric can request that his or her case be heard in ecclesiastical Interjurisdictional court. If the denomination allows this to happen, the case is heard. If the case is heard the denomination must understand that at this level the court, not the Church, decides on the guilt or innocence of the cleric that is final. Based on that decision a recommendation by the court concerning the disposition of the cleric is made. The Church may choose to accept or reject the court recommendation.

If the court decides that the *irregularity* is not warranted and the evidence shows this, the church must remove the *irregularity* and if the cleric was not allowed to receive Holy Orders, the Church has the right to decide if they want to grant that candidate Holy Orders based on the recommendation of the court. It is also the Church's right not to grant Holy Orders because Holy Orders are not a right, but a privilege.

If the cause of the *irregularity* is a serious and notorious issue and has already been brought to the forefront of the Presiding Bishop, Ordinary or Ecclesiastical Court, this can only be dealt with in the External ("public") forum. This cannot be decided behind closed doors. A *notorious* offense is a publicly known or alleged offense. An illustration would be the priest or seminarian accused of sexual relations outside of wedlock (consensual between two adults not abusive or harmful) when the law clearly states this is not allowed, and people in the local parish community know of the affair. If this is the case, then there needs to be an external investigation done on both sides the defense and prosecution, and all the evidence needs to be brought forward and dealt with through the ecclesiastical court.

Dispensing in the Internal Forum

If the offense causing the *irregularities* are in the *occult* (hidden/secret) *irregularity*, the second option of review and/or trial through the *internal forum* may take place.

Some offenses that are made causing the *irregularity*, for the betterment of both the Church and the Parish Community may be best adjudicated internally. This does not abdicate the church's responsibility or the defendant's responsibility to utilize the ecclesiastical court system. In fact, it may be recommended that Interjurisdictional Canon Lawyers should be used to assist in the adjudication of inter-cases to ensure not only the due process of law but that nothing is covered up and all the evidence is presented, and a resolution is made within the confines of the church with the public not knowing a thing about the case at hand. If the resolution of the conflict is done appropriately to protect the good name or reputation of the individual, the internal forum is used. If a person's conscience is at stake and it is not detrimental to the good of the community, the internal forum is used. Where this would not apply is if the clergyperson is accused of child abuse or a notorious crime. That, regardless of conscience or goodness of name, should be brought into the external forum.

In the event that the person becomes aware of an *irregularity* that he or she did not realize may be an *irregularity* that is brought into the internal forum for resolution and dispensation. If the person confesses the sin that caused the irregularity, without breaching the seal of confession, a request can be made using the Interjurisdictional lawyer to write a petition to the competent authority to remove the *irregularity* and all that has to be revealed is that the cleric with good intent can conscience confessed the sin causing the *irregularity*, that sin has been absolved, and the *irregularity* should be considered for removal. If the sin was confessed earlier, before the individual even considered Holy Orders, and was absolved of that sin, and he or she had no idea that that sin constituted the *irregularity (ignorance of the irregularity)*, the person has two choices for the resolution of the *irregularity*. The first choice is to have it dispensed by the Ordinary or Presiding Bishop. The second is to have the case heard in ecclesiastical court with both sides presenting evidence and have the case decided there. Be careful if the case is taken to ecclesiastical court. Remember that decision is final. If you, the Interjurisdictional Canon Layer, after deposing the case, feel that the individual would have a better chance with a dispensation from the Ordinary as opposed to the Ecclesiastical Court, recommend to your client that he or she go to the Ordinary for the dispensation. This may resolve a lot of problems in the future. If the courts decide that person is guilty and should not be admitted into Holy Orders, a recommendation is made to the Church authority and that may change the minds of the hierarchy who at first glance would have dispensed the *irregularity*.

When requesting a dispensation from any *irregularity*, it is always a good idea to have a letter from the cleric's spiritual director or confessor write a letter requestion the dispensation. Again, caution here! The seal of confession is sacred and is not to be broken, so if a letter is written by the confessor or spiritual director, it needs to be to the point with relevant reasons for the dispensation without revealing what was said in the confessional, including implying in the letter what was said in the confessional. The letter should be made out to whoever is in charge of pressing the charges. It may be a Diocesan Bishop, an Administrator, a Chancery Judicial Official, the Presiding Bishop, or another entity of that denomination. Again, the letter must include what brought about the *irregularity* and the judgment, with rationale, of the spiritual director or confessor, addressing the suitability of the person to receive Holy Orders.

Regardless of who writes the letter, the letter is **never to be sent via electronic mail.** Due to the sensitive nature of the issue, could you imagine if the reason or even the *irregularity* went viral? That can cause a great amount of irreputable damage to both the church and the person. The letter should be typed. Preferably the writer should use Times New Roman print and it must be on the appropriate Letter Head of the individual writing. If the person is a church official with an official seal the letter should be, as always, hand signed with the seal of the person included. The letter should also be signed for upon delivery and signed only by the person to whom the letter is written to.

If a person has been approved for Holy Orders, but as of yet has not received the Sacrament, and there is an *irregularity* abound, that is the time the letter should be written and sent out. The sooner the better. This way, all receiving parties of those who are requesting the dispensation are aware that those who have examined the candidate for Holy Orders know about the *irregularity* and have supervised the process and procedure of nullification of the *irregularity* through the appropriate means (confession, spiritual directions, or some other means), and they believe that the *irregularity* should be removed. Once this is done, that letter will be scrutinized by the appropriate dispensing parties (Diocesan Bishop, Archbishop, Presiding Bishop, etc.), and the decision will be sent to the writer of the requesting letter (the superior, the confessor, the spiritual director, the formation director, etc.). Once the letter is received, that letter will be presented to the candidate for Holy Orders and the decision will be read. If the decision is in favor of the candidate and the *irregularity* is removed, the ordination goes forward. If it goes against the individual, then the option to appeal the decision, if warranted, can be made directly to the denying party to reconsider, or to take it to the next level which is the Ecclesiastical Interjurisdictional Court. If the appeal is heard internally and the persons concerned with the staying of the *irregularity* and penalties attached, choose to keep their decision final, then the decision is final and no longer may be appealed. If it goes to court the final decision of the court is final and a recommendation is made to *hold* the *irregularity* and the person does not get Ordained or *stay* the *irregularity* and it is removed. Nonetheless, the final decision to ordain or not ordain is left to the Church administrators. That decision is final and cannot be appealed.

In Conclusion

It must be remembered that everyone has the right to a good name and reputation. Everyone has the right, if Baptized, to receive the sacraments with the exception of Holy Orders. This is the only Sacrament that is not a right but a privilege. This includes the office of Bishop, Archbishop, Presiding Bishop, Primate Archbishop, Chief Administrator, or whatever the church calls those who are ordained.

Holy Orders are based on one's calling from God and their desire to serve and not be served. Even with this calling, the church has a duty to examine each and every candidate for Holy Orders to ensure the safety of the faithful and the church. Many may be called, but few are chosen. There are a lot of mental illnesses, narcissism, predatory behaviors, abusive behaviors, and people who say they have a calling and when it is discovered that their calling came from themselves and not God, they get disappointed, angry, and blame everyone except themselves for the *irregularities* that may come about. Therefore, it is best to have everyone seeking Holy Orders be well scrutinized and examined to ensure the discerning call is a God-given gift.

References

Akers Chart of Collateral & Lineal Relatives with Degree of Kinship: Retrieved from: file:///C:/Users/bisho/OneDrive/Desktop/CHART%20-%20Akers%20Chart%20of%20Collateral%20and%20Lineal%20Relatives%20with%20Degree%20of%20Kinship.pdf. Date Retrieved 5/28/2022.

Apologetics Press (2022). Who Can Baptize Another Person. Retrieved from: https://apologeticspress.org/who-can-baptize-another-person-766/ . Date Retrieved: 5/14/2022

Boudinhon, A. (1910). Canonical Impediments. In <u>The Catholic Encyclopedia</u>. New York: Robert Appleton Company. Retrieved May 24, 2022 from New Advent: <u>http://www</u>. Newadvent.org/cathen/07695a.htm

Canon Law Society of America (CLSA), (1985). The Code of Canon Law. A Text and Commentary. Canon Law Society of America, Washington, DC

Canon Law Society of America (CLSA), (1993). The Code of Canon Law. Canon Law Society of America, Washington, DC

Catholic Encyclopedia (Retrieved, 2006). Irregularity. Retrieved from: (www.newadvent.org/cathen/08170a.htm). www.newadvent.org: Date retrieved: 2022-06-01

Church of the Holy Cross, Dover, DE. (Retrieved 2022) *"What is it that Prevents a Marriage from Being a Marriage?"*, Retrieved from: http://holycrossdover.org/worshipping-god-/sacraments/1054-what-is-it-that-prevents-a-marriage-from-being-a marriage-1054-1054-1054). Date Retrieved: 5/27/2022

Coogan, Michael David (2007). Coogan, Michael David; Brettler, Marc Zvi; Newsom, Carol Ann; Perkins, Pheme (eds.). *The New Oxford Annotated Bible with the Apocryphal/Deuterocanonical Books: New Revised Standard Version, Issue 48* (Augmented 3rd ed.). Oxford University Press. pp. 180–181 New Testament. ISBN [9780195288810](9780195288810).

Dictionary: Illicit, (Retrieved, 2022). *Illicit.* Retrieved from www.catholicculture.org. Date Retrieved, 5/24/22

Dictionary: Invalidity, (Retrieved, 2022). *Invalidity.* Retrieved from www.catholicculture.org. Date Retrieved, 5/24/22

Dictionary: Liceity, (Retrieved, 2022). *Liceity.* Retrieved from www.catholicculture.org. Date Retrieved, 5/24/22

Dictionary: Validity, (Retrieved, 2022). *Validity.* Retrieved from www.catholicculture.org. Date Retrieved, 5/24/22

Doyle, T. (1985). "Marriage". CLSA The Code of Canon Law: A Text and Commentary, pp 737-833.

Ehrensperger, Kathy, (2009). Paul and the Dynamics of Power-3rd Ed., 129-130. Library of New Testament Studies. ISBN: PB:978-0-567-61494-0 in Chow, Chak Him. "Paul's Divergence from Jesus' Prohibition of Divorce in 1 Corinthians 7:10–16" *Open Theology*, vol. 7, no. 1, 2021, pp. 169-179. https://doi.org/10.1515/opth-2020-0157

English Standard Version Bible. (2001). ESV Online. https://esv.literalword.com/

Fanning, W. (1910). *Irregularity.* In *The Catholic Encyclopedia.* New York: Robert Appleton Company. Retrieved May 15,2022, from New Advent: http://www.newadvent.org/cathen/0817a.htm

Garner, B. A., & Black, H. C. (2009). *Black's law dictionary.* 9th ed. St. Paul, MN: West.

Guthrie, Donald (1994). "John". In Carson, D. A.; France, R. T.; Motyer, J. A.; Wenham, G. J. (eds.). New Bible Commentary: 21st Century Edition (4, illustrated, reprint, revised ed.). Inter-Varsity Press. pp. 1021–1065. ISBN 9780851106489.

Hahn, Scott W.; Scott, David (2008). Temple and Contemplation: God's Presence in the Cosmos, Church, and Human Heart. Emmaus Road Publishing. p. 140. ISBN 978-1-931018-52-4.

Hayes, Adam (reviewed by Chip Stapleton), (2022). *Undue Influence.* Laws & Regulations. Crime &Fraud. In Investopedia Retrieved from: https://www.investopedia.com/terms/u/undue-influence.asp. Date Retrieved: 5/29/2022

Hueles, OSM, JCD, John M., (1986). The Pastoral Companion: A Canon Law Handbook for Catholic Ministry, Chicago, The Franciscan Herold Press

Kieffer, René (2007). "60. John". In Barton, John; Muddiman, John (eds.). The Oxford Bible Commentary (first (paperback) ed.). Oxford University Press. pp. 960–1000. ISBN 978-0199277186. Retrieved February 6, 2019.

Killoran, Grant, (Retrieved 2022). *What does it mean to litigate a civil case?*Neil Cannon, Hollman DeLong&Laing, S.C., Retrieved from:

https://www.wilaw.com/mean-litigate-civil-case/?print=pdf. Date Retrieved: 5/10/2022.

Köstenberger, Andreas J. (2004). *John*. Baker Exegetical Commentary on the New Testament. Vol. 4 (illustrated ed.). Baker Academic.
p. 576. ISBN 9780801026447.

Legal Information Institute (Retrieved, 2022). *Alternate Disputes Resolution*. Cornell Law School. Retrieved from: https://www.law.corness.edu/wex/alternative-_disputes_resolution. Date Retrieved: 5/11/2022.

Lombard, Peter & Giulio Silano (2010). The Sentences (Complete in 4 Volumens.) Monee, IL. Amazon-KDP Publishers.

Markham, William, (2006). *How to litigate a lawsuit*. From the Law Offices of William Markham, P.C., Retrieved from: https://www.markhamlawfirm.com/law-articles/san-diego-litigation-attorney/. Date Retrieved: 5/10/2022.

Merriam-Webster. (n.d.). Defendant. In *Merriam-Webster.com dictionary*. Retrieved May 15, 2022, from https://www.merriam-webster.com/dictionary/defendant

Quroa, (Retrieved 2022). *I want to become a Baptist, however, I was baptized as an infant in an Orthodox Church?* Retrieved from: on (https://www.quora.com/I-want-to-become-a-Baptist-however-I-was-baptized-as-an-infant-in-Orthodox-church-Will-I-be-rebaptized-when-entering-Baptist-Church). Date Retrieved: 5/14/2022.

Redeemer. (1996). What's the History of Christian Baptism? Retrieved on 27 Sept, 2012 from: http://myredeemer.org/foundation/baptism/history.shtml

Reese, Thomas, (2020-09-15). *Vatican causes chaos by invalidating baptism formula.* Religion News Service. Retrieved from https://www.ncronline.org/news/theology/signs-times/vatican-causes-chaos-invalidating-baptism-formula. Date Retrieved: 2022-25-05

Richert, Scott P, (2019). *Learning Religions. What is a Sacrament? A Lesson inspired by the Baltimore Catechism.* Retrieved from: https://www.learnreligions.com/what-is-a-sacrament-541717#:~:text=A%20sacrament%20is%20a%20symbolic,parishioner%20by%20a%20priest%20or. Date Retrieved: 5/13/2022

Richert, Scott P. (2021, February 16). What Is a Sacrament? Retrieved from https://www.learnreligions.com/what-is-a-sacrament-541717

Scuderi, Archbishop Anthony J, (2002). *Interjurisdictional Canon Law- Volume 4 – Sacraments, Sanctions and Process Issues.* Monee, IL, Amazon KDP Publishers

Scuderi, Archbishop Anthony J, (2002). *Interjurisdictional Canon Law- Volume 1 – Introduction to Interjurisdictional Canon Law for the Independent and Ecumenical Catholic Churches.* Monee, IL, Amazon KDP Publishers

Scuderi, Archbishop Anthony J. (2022), *A Text, Commentary and Canon Law of the Ecumenical Catholic Church of Christ-Worldwide.* Monee, IL, Amazon KDP Publishers.

Simpson, John on Quora (Retrieved 2022), https://www.quora.com/I-want-to-become-a-Baptist-however-I-was-baptized-as-an-infant-in-Orthodox-church-Will-I-be-rebaptized-when-entering-Baptist-Church.

The Forgiveness of Sins. Retrieved from: https://www.catholic.com/tract/the-forgiveness-of-sins. Date Retrieved: 2/20/21

Wilkerson, Jennifer, L. (Retrieved 2022). The Czech Republic and Consanguinity-August 31, 2015. Jennifer L. Wilkerson, A Professional Corporaton, Attorney at Law. Retrieved from: http://www.jwilkerson.net/the-czech-republic-and-consanguinity/. Date Retireved: 5/29/22

Young, John (1996). Christianity. McGraw-Hill. p. 113. ISBN 978-0-8442-3116-7.

Canon Law Dictionary to Volume 4

Made in the USA
Columbia, SC
08 April 2023

d1eec03a-ee2d-49b0-a806-aefa3d6f2676R01